NIGERIAN ARABIC-ENGLISH DICTIONARY

BIBLIOTHECA AFROASIATICA

Editor: Robert Hetzron

Assistant Editor: John Hayes

VOLUME TWO

Undena Publications

Malibu 1986

NIGERIAN ARABIC-ENGLISH DICTIONARY

by

Alan S. Kaye

Nigerian Arabic-English Dictionary is the companion volume to the author's *A Dictionary of Nigerian Arabic*, which was published in 1982 (*Bibliotheca Afroasiatica,* Volume 1). It lists the approximately 6,000 lexemes with some illustrative sentences alphabetically from Arabic to English using the same transcription as the 1982 volume. Although most Arabic dictionaries are organized under a triconsonantal root, the loss of laryngeals and pharyngeals as well as other developments have brought about a "mutilated" root situation. Therefore, it was decided to arrange the data alphabetically rather than under a historical root. This dictionary is geared to be of use to the specialist in comparative Arabic dialectology and Semitic linguistics as well as to the general linguist interested in Afroasiatic data from a synchronic point of view. In addition, the volume will be of interest to the Africanist dealing with linguistic diffusion and borrowing. The present study is a product of the author's 1973-1974 field work in Northern Nigeria, sponsored by the National Endowment for the Humanities, the American Philosophical Society and the Research Committee of California State University, Fullerton.

Library of Congress Card Number: 81-71736

ISBN: 0-89003-191-6/paper

0-89003-190-8/cloth

Undena Publications, P.O. Box 97, Malibu, CA 90265, U.S.A.

PREFACE

This is the companion volume to my *A Dictionary of Nigerian Arabic* (1982), which was published in hardback as well as paperback by Undena Publications, Malibu, California (they are also the publishers of the journal *Afroasiatic Linguistics*). The present work was finished in 1982 and scheduled to appear in 1983; however, circumstances beyond my control have unfortunately delayed publication until now. The 1982 volume was English-Nigerian Arabic; this, its sister volume, is Nigerian Arabic-English.

The reviews of the 1982 volume (in *Language, Al-ʿArabiyya: Journal of the American Association of Teachers of Arabic, The Journal of African Languages and Linguistics,* etc.) have clearly demonstrated that Nigerian Arabic studies are part of a new interest generated in the lesser known dialects of vernacular Arabic (such as the Anatolian dialects, the dialects of Saudi Arabia and the Gulf countries, the Yemens, Chad, Khuzestan, Afghanistan and the U.S.S.R., and Juba Arabic of Equatoria Province in the southern Sudan, originally a pidgin but now a creole and its closely related Ki-Nubi [Arabic] of Kenya and Uganda). Since this volume's potential readership will be linguists, dialectologists, anthropologists, sociologists, and other specialists within the humanities and social sciences, rather than people with more practical interests and motives such as tourists, the book is structured accordingly.

The 1982 volume sets forth, in the introductory sections, information about the field techniques used to elicit and gather the corpus as well as remarks concerning the phonology and grammar of Nigerian Arabic. The reader is here referred to those pages.

The diachronic development of Nigerian Arabic is very striking to the expert in other Arabic dialects when these are seen in terms of the total picture of the development of western Sudanese Arabic dialects, viz., the dialects of Dar Fur (e.g., El Fasher), Kordofan, and Bahr El Ghazal, which have also, together with northern dialects, produced Juba Arabic and Ki-Nubi (Arabic), sometimes just called Nubi (no relationship with Nubian). Indeed I am now in the process of studying those two Arabic dialects in order to comprehend the diachronic developments in Nigerian Arabic and, of course, in the closely related Arabic dialects of Chad (cf. my *Chadian and Sudanese Arabic in the Light of Comparative Arabic Dialectology,* The Hague and Paris: Mouton and Co., 1976, for further information as well as bibliography). For instance, classical Arabic /q/ can have a reflex in Nigerian Arabic as /q/, /ʾ/, /g/, or /ɣ/ (among other developments), and many originally epenthetic vowels have become fully phonemic, as in *akibar* 'better' or *akinas* 'worse', where the second vowels are the anaptyctic ones inserted to break up consonant clusters. I hope to fully investigate these diachronic developments in my future work. It is worthwhile noting here that historical epenthesis has very little or nothing at all to do with a phonemic transcription. Thus, for instance, when an English loanword like *school* is borrowed into Hindi-Urdu, it comes out either as /sikuul/ or /ʾiskuul/ and must be so written! Also, in Arabic a form like Cairene /ħaʾʾúku/ 'your right' (m. pl.) even indicates that an historically-motivated epenthetic vowel may acquire the primary word stress. These happenings are worthy, by themselves, of monographic exploration.

A few words regarding the organization of the following pages of this dictionary may prove helpful. Since my departure point is the 1982 volume, all words, forms, and sentences used there have been put in alphabetical order here. There are thus a very large number of sentences beginning with *ana* 'I'. This has both advantages and disadvantages. On the one hand, it is possible to investigate a great number of basic sentence types such as equational sentences or the use of pre-verbs such as *garrab* in *addūd garrab bumūt* 'The lion nearly died'. On the other hand, a linguist would, most probably, expect to find such sentences elsewhere, viz., under *garrab* or *māt, bumūt* 'to die'. Hopefully, this practice will not cause a troublesome search for a lexeme or morpheme.

In authoring any dictionary, the lexicographer must make practical decisions and they have to be made many times over on every page. I have come to realize that lexicography, in particular, more than other types of linguistic work, requires the most painstaking efforts simply due to all the decisions which one is obliged to make. Probably no dictionary compiler anywhere or at any time could have predicted the underestimated amount of time and extra expenditures of money and effort which have gone into its production, yet the work is necessary and extremely satisfying and rewarding when once accomplished.

Of course, at one time, for ease of reference, I contemplated cross-referencing the illustrative sentences bilexemically so that they could be located in at least two places in the dictionary. To save space, however, this was rarely possible. I am the first one to admit that a larger dictionary *should* do this (where space is not so constrained).

I am also well aware of the fact that some lexicographers would have preferred to list the inflectional forms of a particular lexeme under its so-called "main entry." However, this would have introduced much needless complication into the "main entry." Besides, looking at Juba Arabic and Ki-Nubi, to compare as parallels, very often an (historical) imperative (pl.) has become the "main entry" verb. Thus in Juba Arabic *ana šilu sakiin min mara* 'I took a knife from the woman', the verb *šilu* 'took' derives, etymologically, from the pl. imperative (= Modern Standard Arabic *šīlū*, spelled < šylw >). Or *rajil de der alabu* 'The man wants to play', *alabu* 'play' derives from *ʾalʿabu* 'play!' (m. pl. imp.), the first vowel of which is *i* and the final vowel of which is long in Modern Standard Arabic (the *i* vowel and the glottal stop elide in non-initial position anyway).

It is very true that *agif* 'stop!' is related to *wagaf* ~ *wigif* ~ *wifig, bigīf* 'stop!' (intr.), and *waggaf, biwaggif* 'stop' (tr.), *wafka* ~ *wakfa* 'pause, wait (n.)', but at some point the *Sprachgefühl* of the native speaker fails to associate lexemes under the "root." For instance, would a native speaker of English want to be obliged to look up the word "junction" or "juncture" under "joint," or "point" and "puncture" both under "point?" Furthermore, is this practice desirable? Sometimes, it is more useful, especially in the reading of texts, to have a listing for *am, is, were, be,* etc., rather than have all of these inflectional forms only occurring under "be" as the basic form/main entry.

I wrestled at first with the idea of listing words under the *historical* triconsonantal root (if known), but soon I became disenchanted with this idea because, synchronically, the triconsonantal root could have become MUTILATED, as is the case elsewhere in modern Semitic as with the Ethiopic languages. For example, the root of Harari *kūd* 'liver' is *kbd,* but the *b* manifests itself in the long vowel. This also happens in Hebrew, to cite a parallel in another Semitic language, in which *latet* 'to give' derives from the root *ntn* (only the *t* shows up in this particular form). Therefore, I felt that I had no choice but to list things under an alphabetical ordering. Thus, the word *ʾalme* 'water' could not be listed under *m* (= Modern Standard Arabic *māʾ*) since the lexeme never occurs without *ʾal,* which is an historically frozen definite article in Nigerian Arabic. The form *me* does not exist, but *ʾalʾalme* does. Thus, it is hoped that the user of this dictionary will not look under the wrong place for a lexeme's occurrence. However, since the 1982 sister volume can be used as a co-reference, I hope any possible inconvenience will be minimal.

The practice described above is the more defensible since neither this dictionary nor the

1982 volume is etymological. To the linguist, some lexemes have very obvious etymologies such as *bel,* (pl.) *bīlān* 'belt', which in fact, derive from English 'belt' through final consonant cluster reduction. But I decided, years before the 1982 volume was published, to save etymological work as well as any thorough diachronic investigations until last. In the meantime, Lethem (1920) provides some useful etymologies, and a linguist interested in this area is wise to check into the dictionaries of Kanuri (Kanembu) and Hausa, where some obvious source words will be found (e.g., *yáwwā́* or *yawwā* 'fine, OK, . . .' < Hausa). While I would have liked nothing better than to add etymologies, at least for the foreign vocabulary recognizable to me, this lies beyond the scope of the present work.

It is imperative that I now comment on some editorial practices that have direct relevance to the pages which follow, in that they will allow for a correct reading and/or interpretation of the data.

1. I have decided to hyphenate reduplicative expressions such as *ām-ʾām* 'two years ago' rather than list (without a hyphen) as in the 1982 volume. I have also done this in various compounds such as *arbaʾa-ʾalif* 'four thousand'. Furthermore, sometimes I have hyphenated merely for the sake of typographical convenience, e.g., *barak* 'kneel down' followed by ____*-atak* 'Greetings!'. Very often, one is aware of a common root when this technique is utilized.

2. I have decided to be somewhat pleonastic and tautological (in the hopes of avoiding ambiguity) in, e.g., forms like *ambala, bimbali* (i.e., the imperfect), ____ (*b-*) 'disappoint', 'be disappointed in' rather than take a chance on the assumption that a reader might not know that the *b-*, which is optional anyhow, often collocates with the main verb.

3. There are some technical errors which have been left as is (for typographical convenience as well as to save space). Thus *gassa, buguss* 'cut open, cut one's finger, skin' occurs in the idiom *gassa lxabar* 'cut one's story short', but its corresponding imperfect should read *buguss alxabar* rather than *buguss lxabar*, in which the *a-* of the definite article should be correctly inserted by the automatic morphophonemic rules of the language. Hopefully, this will cause little or no confusion/inaccuracy.

4. With verbs and nouns in the actual utterances (illustrative sentences), the underscore refers *only* to the first form given (i.e., sg. for nouns and pf. for verbs).

5. The optional emphatics are alphabetized as if emphatic.

6. The glottal stop has been alphabetized as occurring between the letters *h* and *i.* Since the glottal stop and *h* are both laryngeals, it was decided to alphabetize them next to each other.

7. Preparing this volume has made me aware of a few errors in the 1982 volume (not caught, incidentally, by any of the reviewers, at least so far). For instance, *mastará* (not listed in the 1982 volume) 'grave' is listed here, with its pl. *masātir*, which normally means 'graveyard', i.e., '(place of many) graves'. As a corollary to this admission, I believe most dictionary authors/editors/compilers are better aware of their finished product's inadequacies than the most critical reviewers and/or users.

8. See the 1982 volume for bibliography and general observations on the dictionary.

After work on this volume is completed, I plan to return to my book of texts (collected during 1973-74 and transcribed from tape recordings) with grammatical notes and description. I have been working on these texts for more than a decade now, but regrettably, I am a slow worker (no apologies solicited here) and often get sidetracked by other projects, which are probably less important but just as interesting and rewarding.

Finally, it is incumbent upon me to thank the publishers, with whom it has been a pleasure to work, and the members of my family: my wife, Susan, and our children, Jennifer and Jeremy, with all of whom I should have spent more time.

Alan S. Kaye
Fullerton, Californa
July 1984

ABBREVIATIONS OF GRAMMATICAL TERMINOLOGY

act.	=	active	lit.	=	literal(ly)
adj.	=	adjective	m.	=	masculine
adv.	=	adverb	n.	=	noun
anat.	=	anatomical	orn.	=	ornithological
anim.	=	animate	part.	=	participle
assim.	=	assimilated	pf.	=	perfect
bot.	=	botanical	pl.	=	plural
coll.	=	collective	pls.	=	plurals
colls.	=	collectives	prep.	=	preposition
comm. pl.	=	common plural	pron.	=	pronominal
conj.	=	conjunction	pro.	=	pronoun
d.o.	=	direct object	p.n.	=	proper noun
d.	=	dual	refl.	=	reflexive
ds.	=	duals	rel.	=	relative
f.	=	feminine	sg.	=	singular
gen.	=	generic	s.o.	=	someone
imp.	=	imperative	s.t.	=	something
impf.	=	imperfect	suff.	=	suffix
inan.	=	inanimate	tr.	=	transitive
i.o.	=	indirect object	v.	=	verb
interr.	=	interrogative	v.n.	=	verbal noun
intr.	=	intransitive	zool.	=	zoological

A

ab digin bearded man

abā, biyāba refuse, resign

abad, be'abad worship (v.)

abarbá, (coll.) *abarba* pineapple

abarbar(a) dust

abāṭ, (ds.)*ubuṭēn* ~ *abuṭ 'itnēn,* (pl.) *ubuṭṭe* armpit

abba dad(dy) [typical child's nickname]

abda 'algrā min jadīd Start studying again!

abi 'ēn angawīye one who has big eyes

abi šōk porcupine

abikam, bakma, abkamīn, -āt mute

abin dannān (sg./pl.) wasp
 ____ *fišfāš* (sg./pl.) lung
 ____ *šabbāš* ~ *šabaš/k* (no pl.) spider
 ____ *tassās* heartburn, indigestion

abi/ungurdān (sg./pl.) tick

abir, (pl.) *ubūr* grape

ablam, balma, (pl.) *bulum* retarded, stupid, idiot(ic)

abōbá, (coll.) *abōbo* pumpkin

ábu, (pl.) *abbahāt* father
 ____ *darag* kind of snake
 ____ *garn* rhinoceros
 ____ *luxlux* pelican
 ____ *mūs* type of fish
 ____ *naṭwāt* bat (zool.)
 ____ *nusēn* fox
 ____ *riyēs* migraine (headache)
 ____ *ṣabūr,* (f.) *amm ṣabūr* patient person
 ____ *xadīja* nickname for hyena
 ____ *xarīṭe* stork
 ____ *xarṭūm, an xarṭūm* (no. pl.) very tall
 ____ *xordāfa* hunchback

abū his father

abu/inguda (no pl.) turtle, tortoise

abunkunni earring(s)

(*abun*) *sarrār* (no pl.) cricket

abyaḍ, bēḍa, (pl.) *buyuḍ* white
 ____ *tall/karr* snow white, very white

abzar, fazra, abzarīn, fazrāt swayback

ačakčak, bičakčak tiptoe

āda, bi'āda infect (tr.)

ādá, -āt custom

adad, (pl.) *idād* number

adal, bēdil make s.o. stand straight and upright or in ready-position

adāla justice

adalla Climb down!

adam algudra inability
 ____ *aššukur* ingratitude

adār very tall grass by a river

adāra, -āt injury

adda, bi'a/eddi cross, cut across, ford
 ____, *bi'idd* count

addab, bi'addib discipline, punish

addābar, biddābar keep one's money for a pension

addabbar, biddabbar arrange

addaffa, biddaffa sit around a fire

addāgaš, biddāgaš butt one another

ad(da)'a, bid(d)e'i pray

addal, bi'addil clean, repair, decorate

addāl, -īn repairman

addālal, biddālal play

addalla, biddalla go down a slope, slope down

addar, bi'addir injure

addargas, biddargas roll down, under or off, slide off (intr.)

addārīye later

addarra, biddarra go slowly

addāwas, biddāwis fight, quarrel

addayyan, biddayyan borrow

addini any, every
  ___ *nādum birīd gabīla* They like each other.
  ___ *sabāh* every morning
  ___ *subū* " "
  ___ *yōm kalām dunya gā'id bas* Every day there is a lot of trouble.

addinye/a hāmiye It's hot.

addinya/e qāmat It's cloudy.

addōdal, biddōdal hang, be suspended

addōra 'alfātit last week
  ___ *ttiji* next week

addunya future [Cf. *dunya*]
  ___ (*bigat*) *fillēl* It's night.
  ___ *'amsat,* ___ *timsa* become dark (weather)
  ___ *'aṣabat* It's morning.

addūt garrab bumūt The lion nearly died.

adil justice

adīl, -e, -īn, -āt straight and upright, right, correct, candid, honest, just, righteous

ādil ~ *adīl, -e, -īn, -āt* just (adj.)

adilān, -a, -īn, -āt just (adj.)

ādilan righteousness

adu (sg./pl.) enemy

aduxul Come inside!

adwaš, -īn quick-tempered

aḍalam, biḍalam become dark

aḍḍa, bi'aḍḍi bite (v.)

aḍḍamman, biḍḍamman guarantee, give security

aḍḍeyyef, biḍḍeyyef become a guest

aḍum, (pl.) *i/uḍām* bone
  ___ *addigin,* (pls.) ___ *addūgun* jawbone
  ___ *aṣṣaff* rib

āfa, bēfa forgive
  ___ *l-* apologize
  ___ *lēna* We apologize.
  ___ *ley* I apologize. Forgive me!

afa/ina (no pl.) smell (n.)

āfāni Forgive me!

afar, bi'afar forgive

āf(a)rat (no pl.) white cloud

affan, bi'affin smell bad

af'ala gadé Do it again!

āfi (all genders/numbers) healthy, safe, well, great, fine (response to greetings)
  ___ *bas* I am simply fine.
  ___ *ley* very well, very fine
  ___ *sile* quite good, quite well
  ___ *ṭayy(i)bīn* (response to greetings)

afkur ṭayyib l- beware
  ___ *-alkalb* beware of the dog!

afrīt, (pl.) *afārīt* demon

āfuno Hausa (language and people)

agab, bēgib pass, go by

agāb remainder, rest

agaban ago

agad, bēgid ~ *bi'egda* tie, knot

agdar fi qaši/amak Close your mouth! / Shut up!

agegá, (pl.) *ageg* stalk of guinea corn

aggab, bi'aggib pass, take

agīd, (pl.) *agada* partner

agīf Stop! Wait!
  ___ *min alkalām* Stop talking! Be quiet!
  ___ *min alxalbāt* Stop talking nonsense!
  ___ *šiya* Wait a bit!
  ___ *šiya ke* Stop (wait) a little!

agil (no pl.) intelligence, sense

āgil, -e, -īn, -āt intelligent, careful

agila Receive it!
  ___ *'andarab* He was confused.

āgir, -āt barren, childless

agod, agōdi, agōdu, agōdan Sit!
  ____*fi usṭ albēt* Sit in the middle of the room!

agōgo(ʾ)a ~ *agōgo,* (pl.) *agōgāt* clock, watch

agōgōtak kam What time is it?

agrab, (pl.) *agārib* scorpion

aɣabaš, qabša, (pl.) *qubuš* shade of pink

aɣabaš Aqabash [boy's nickname]

āha yes

ahal (no pl.) family

ahalāt albēt furniture

ahali ʾāfi ~ *ahal bēti ʾāfi* My family is fine.

ahlā lēna mā le hinēn We are enjoying that place more than this place.

ahlāʾ min sweeter than

ahmar ~ *ēmar* ~ *eʾmar, hamra,* (pl.) *humur* red, pink

āǰ class, grade (in school)

ajab amazement, wonder, surprise, miracle

aǰāb, biǰawb answer (v.)

aǰābad, biǰābad pull s.o. to
  ____ (*fōg*) bargain over s.t.

aǰāǰ dust

aǰal- + pron. suff. may
  ____ *-a bilwarma/yamūt* May he die!
  ____ *-ak helū lēk* May you be happy!
  ____ *-ak tamūt* May you die!

aǰala fast, quickly, hurriedly, immediately

aǰami, aǰamīye, aǰamīn, aǰam(īy)āt ignorant, not knowing Arabic

aǰar, bēǰir rent (v.)

aǰāra rent (n.)

aǰeguma white guinea corn

aǰilus falṭa Sit down!

aǰīne porridge
  ____ *zarga* porridge without milk

aǰir, ____ *balhēl* Run quickly!
  ____ *balʾagil* Run slowly!
  ____ *gadé* Run again!

āǰisān, -a, -īn, -āt very tired, exhausted

aǰǰab, biʾaǰǰib surprise (tr.)

aǰǰar, biʾaǰǰir hire, rent (v.)

aǰǰāwab, biǰǰāwab argue

aǰǰāwad, biǰǰāwad be generous

aǰǰaz, biʾaǰǰiz make s.o. old and tired

aǰǰime ~ *alǰīme* Friday

aǰǰu akanni/gaṭa galbi/gaṭa masārni/katanni I am starving.

ajurá, (coll.) *ajur* reward

aǰūz, (pl.) *aǰāyiz* old woman

aǰzān, -a, -īn, -āt old and tired person

akal, biyākul eat, consume; defeat, win, cheat, swindle
  ____ *alʾintaha* pass an examination
  ____ *giddām* (make) progress

akalna xalās We already ate.

akfa ~ *afka* Turn it upside down!

akibar better, best, nicer, nicest

akil food

ākil, -e, -īn, -āt eaten, eating

akinas worse

akkal, biʾakkil feed

akkāl, -a, -īn, -āt person with a good appetite, good eater, glutton

ākōti box

aksa more difficult

aktar annās majority (of people)

aku (sg./pl.) parrot

al-, (assim. variants) *ad-, aḍ-, aǰ-, an-, ar-, as-, aṣ-, -aš-, at-, aṭ-, az-* (all genders/numbers) (def. art.) the; (rel. pron.) which, what, who(m)

ala/e on

āla, -āt material(s), tool, thing

alafa acquaintance

alam, bēlam (*b-*) know

alam, (pl.) *ālām* banner, mark

alam ~ *qalam,* (pls.) *qulumma/e* ~ *qulūm* ~ *qulmān* pen

alāma, -āt sign (n.)
____*-t almaṭara* sign of rain

alárba'a Wednesday

alāwa ~ *halāwa, -āt* sweets, candy

alawān head of a district

albagar marūdi 'ana I love cows.

albaka, bilbaki cry

albālax, bilbālax (*fōg*) be rude to s.o.

albān ~ *qalbān, -a, -īn, -āt* tired, pregnant

albārak, -i, -u, -an Please!
____ *t(a')āl, -i, -u, -an* Please come!

albāram, bilbāram fight

albardā cold season, harmattan

albāri/e yesterday
____*fillēl* last night

albarra toilet

albarra, bilbarra (*l-*) warn

albarrad, bilbarrad take a bath

albarram, bilbarram gaze; turn over repeatedly

albarsa, bilbarsa have confidence in s.o.

albēt 'asīr The room is private.

albisāṭāṭ ma 'ajabanni I didn't like the carpets.

albišrīk I have good news for you.
[The response to this is *gōro* 'kola nuts,' since one partakes of one before revealing the news.]

albitt bāyre The girl has no lover.

albukān ḍāka dabba mā lehinēn That place is higher than the one here.

alériya aerial, antenna

alf thousand
____ *-ēn* two thousand
____ *wāhid* one thousand

alfaḍḍal, bilfaḍḍal be left over
____, *-i, -u, -an* Please!

alfakī rama lēhum al'āyāt The teacher dictated the Koranic verses to them.

alfakkar, bilfakkar think, consider, remember

alfarraš, bilfarraš sit, spread out (comfortably)

alfassa, bilfassa be eloquent or skillful

alfāt past (n.)

alfātan, bilfātan quarrel

algāji, -ye, -yīn, -yāt smallest, youngest; little finger

algamar xanagō The moon eclipsed.

algāsam, bilgāsam ~ *bilgisim* divide

algāsar, bilgāsar (*falṭa*) squat, stoop

algaṭṭa, bilgaṭṭa cover onself with s.t., cover with clothes

algumnati government

alhaddas, bilhaddas be told

alhadīde anṭabagat The iron bent.

alhaḍḍar, bilhaḍḍar prepare oneself, be on guard

alhāji, (pl.) *(al)hujjāj alhajji* (lit., one who has made the pilgrimage to Mecca; usually, however, a title of respect)

alhajja, bilhajja talk, converse

alhajya Alhajya (p.n.f.)

alhakar, bilhakar sit with legs crossed

alhamdu/i lillāhi Praise be to God!

alhammad, bilhammad thank God

alhangat, bilhangat have hunger pains

alhāraj, bilhāraj fight or quarrel with one another

alharrag, bilharrag be burned, roasted

alharrak, bilharrak be moved

alharram, bilharram be respected

alhawāss alxamsa the five senses

alhaxx fōgak It's your fault.

alhazza, bilhazza mock, ridicule, make fun of

alhelū gāʾid It was pleasurable.

alʾaḍḍar, bilʾaḍḍar prevent oneself

alʾāfa, bilʾāfa get better or cured, improve (health)

alʾāfi safety

alʾajjab, bilʾajjab be amazed, surprised

alʾallag, bilʾallag be hung

(alʾ)alme water

alʾām alfāt last year

alʾammal, bilʾammal be ready

alʾānas, bilʾānas converse
 ___ *(fi)* discuss
 ___ *(maʾa)* spend time talking with s.o.

alʾanna, bilʾanna groan

alʾāraṭ, bilʾāraṭ inherit

alʾāša, bilʾāša eat dinner (with)

alʾašša, bilʾašša " " "

alʾaṭwal tallest

alʾāwaṭ, bilʾāwaṭ shout, yell

alʾaxxar, bilʾaxxar come late

alʾēb sawwāha She felt shameful.

alʾinglīzīya English language

alʾislām Islam

alʾusub, ___ *alkabīr* thumb
 ___ *allubbāni* middle finger
 ___ *assaʾīr algāǰi* little finger, pinkie
 ___ *aṭṭawīl* middle finger
 ___ *hana rriǰil* toe

ālik however

alim kind of tree (planted near mosques)

ālim, ālma, -īn, -āt clever, intelligent, knowledgeable (person)
 ___, (pl.) *ulamā* learned (person in Islam)

alingilēk, -i, -u, -an Please!
 ___ *ʾagod falṭa* Please sit down!

alitinēn Monday

alkalām alʾadīl justice

alkālam, bilkālam have words with s.o., almost start a fight

alkallam, bilkallam speak
 ___ *balhēl* Speak louder!
 ___ *baṭūl hissak* Speak louder!

alkalwa, bilkalwa console (v.)

alkanǰar, bilkanǰar bend (tr.)

alkāre oil

alkarfas, bilkarfas be(come) wrinkled

alkaršam, bilkaršam wither (intr.), be(come) wrinkled

alkassar, bilkassar be broken

alkūzi hana lladāy kitchen

allaban marūdi ʾana I love milk.

allabbad, billabbad hide (intr.), take cover

allabbas, billabbas dress oneself, get dressed

allag, biʾallig hang (tr.)

allagga, billagga meet

allam, biʾallim teach, educate
 ___, *biʾellem* mention

allām, -īn scholar, great teacher

allamlam, billamlam be collected or gathered together

allamma, billamma be collected or gathered together

allammas, billammas touch

allāsaf, billāsaf be reflected

alle may, must
 ___ *yaǰīb* he must bring
 ___ *yamši* He may go.

allēle tonight
 ___ *nisawwi ʾazumá hīl ʾanǰumma*
 Tonight we will celebrate a holiday.

allēmūná māsxe The lemon is tasteless.

allibrāy labor, work (n.)

allihēd ~ *allahad* ~ *alʾahad* Sunday

allōlab, billōlab swing, wag (tr.)

almā bisidda ttār abū humār He who won't take revenge, his father is a donkey.

almadrasa/almakarantīye al ʾawwal elementary or primary school

almadrasa/almakarantīye ttāniye secondary school

almaktūb, ___ *attawa* the (very) same book
___ *da sāriginna/ansarag* This book is stolen.

almallax, bilmallax play a trick on

almān, -a, -īn, -āt aware

almassa, bilmassa anoint oneself

almaṭara (first big) rain, rainy season
___ *naggaṭat* The rain fell.
___ *tusubb barra hassa* It's raining outside now.

alme water
___ *halawāt* soft drink
___ *helū/ǰadīd* fresh water
___ *lfagara* gruel for the poor
___ *lwuḍū* ablution water
___ *māsax* unadulterated water
___ *mudaffa* boiling or boiled water
___ *sāfi* pure water
___ *tamali* yellow-orange

alme ʾellem biyarf alkatib The teacher knows how to write.

alqadda, bilqadda have breakfast or lunch (together), eat during Ramadan

alqāfar, bilqāfar reconcile

alqālaṭ, bilqālaṭ argue

alqalla, ___ *gammat kubār* The guinea corn grew tall.
___ *kubār* The guinea corn is tall.

alqassal, bilqassal wash one's hands and face

alqurʾān Koran

alūd kind of perfume

alūg ~ *alīge* fodder

alwačwač, bilwačwač reflect

alwaddar, bilwaddir lose (intr.)

alwaḍḍa, bilwaḍḍa perform ablution

alwāǰa, bilwāǰa argue

alwakkal, bilwakkil (*ala*) depend (on)

alwal a boy, some boy or other

alwāla, bilwāla meet one another

alwalda ~ *alwalad da* this boy

alwaqtāt alxamsa the five obligatory prayers

alwattad, bilwattad become firm, stiffen

alwaṭā, ___ *hāmi(ye)* It's hot (weather).
___ *hārr(e)* " " "
___ *ʾamsat,* ___ *timsa* become dark
___ *ʾaṣabat* It's morning.
___ *karba* It's hot and stuffy.
___ *kulla* the whole area
___ *miqayyme* It's cloudy.
___ *qamīme* " "
___ *šāle* The weather is fair.
___ *tuqūm* It's cloudy.
___ *xarīf* ~ *bārde/a* ~ *sāgte* ~ *sākṭe* It's cold.
___ *xarīf/xarrafat* It's the rainy season.

alwayr aerial, antenna

alwēke māsxe The gruel is unseasoned.

alxālaf, bilxālaf disagree, quarrel

alxalbaṭ, bilxalbaṭ be confused

alxamīs Thursday

alxarīf, -āt rainy season

alxarraṭ, bilxarraṭ fall down, roll off

alxāṭaf, bilxāṭaf buy, pay for, shoplift

alxaṭara, bilxaṭara jump over

alxayyar, bilxayyar prefer

alxōf hana ʾaḻḻa fear of God

alxubār some news

alyōm, ___ *alfāt* yesterday
___ *allahad* Sunday

aḻḻa God; Really?
___ *aḻḻa* anxious, very anxious to
___ *āsan lēk* Thank you! (to old people)
___ *bifzāni* God will save me! May God save me!
___ *surfak* God curse you!

___ *yabarkak* Thank you!
___ *yāfīk* May God forgive you!
___ *yafta* ~ *yafta* ___ God will help you. [Said by wives to their husbands in the morning; i.e., 'God will help you find another buyer (or seller).']
___ *yafta(h)* God give us luck!
___ *yagdar fīya* God forbid!
___ *yahfadak* May God keep you! [Said to important people]
___ *yalummuna balxēr* God will meet us in good condition. Good-bye! Farewell!
___ *yanazzalak bal'āfi* (Have a) safe journey!
___ *yasabbīna yāṭīna* Good night!
___ *yasirfak* God damn you!
___ *yaṭawwil 'umrak* May God grant you long life!
___ *yaṭīk algafāra* May God forgive you!
___ *yaṭīk al'ajur* May God reward you!
___ *yawaddīk bal'āfi* May God keep you healthy! Take care! Good-bye!
___ *yawarīna lxēr* God will show us goodness!
___ *yazīd 'imānak* May God increase your faith!
___ *yazīd mālak* May God increase your wealth!
___ *yazīd xērak* God will/May God increase your goodness!
___ *yazīd zamānak* May God increase your time!
___ *yazīdak* (lit.,) May God increase you! May God give you more of everything!
___ *yibārak* Thank God!
___ *yibārak fik/fōgak* Thank you!
___ *yibārikak* May God bless you!
___ *yijawwid hālak* May God renew your state!
___ *yikattir ajurak* God will increase your reward!
___ *yinasrak/yanṣurak* (lit.,) God will make you succeed! May God help you!

am owner
___ *sīlīye* (no pl.) kind of lizard with red body and white lines

ām, (pl.) *awām* year
___ *-'ām* two years ago

ām, bu'ūm swim

āma (m./f.sg.) blind

amal, be'emal do

āmal, biyāmul hex

āman bēk I believe you.

amar, bēmar command

āmar, bi'āmar order s.o.
___, *bi'āmir (l-)* forgive

ambaddi (no pl.) butterfly

ambaddi, ambaddīye, (pl.) *ambadada* beggar who habitually studies the Koran

ambaddi, (pl.) *fa'ara* young adult (approx. 25 years old)

ambākir tomorrow
___ *sabah/subū* tomorrow morning

ambal kind of alcoholic beverage, local brew, beer

ambala, bimbali, ___ *(b-)* disappoint, be disappointed in
___ *(bēn)* provoke s.o. to fight

ambalas, bimbalis fall out or down, get lost

amballa, bimballa be(come) moist or wet

ambaram, bimbarim look; turn over (car engine)

ambaraṭ, bimbariṭ peel off (one's skin)

ambatar, bimbatir be loose

ambaṭa, bimbaṭi lay, be placed on

ambaṭan, bimbaṭin get diarrhea

ambawāla, -āt rain gutters for local-type houses

ambēnat between

(am)bēni haw (am)bēnak between you and me

ambikay, -e, ambáwaka, ambikayāt deaf-mute

ambirbitīye, (coll.) *ambirbiti* frog

ambītēbit sandstorm, white fine dust in hair from sandstorm, haze

amboɣa' Pound/Beat it!

ambuktāy, -e, ambukti, ambúktiyāt hunter living in the bush *ambūku* (m./f.-no pl.) mute [usually a term of address]

amburlum kind of snake

amdihēr disease causing a hump on back

amfakka, bimfakka be sprained

amfirēša back part of animal

amfirihāna epilepsy

amfitfit "

amflētīk, -īn spy (n.)

amfūla kind of grass in water

am(i) šinib woman with lip ring

āmīn Amen!

āmir, āmri, āmrīn, -āt crowded, populated

amīre, -āt crowd (n.)

amis yesterday

amiš, amši, -u, -an Go!
 ___ *ba'aglak* Go slowly/carefully!
 ___ *bal'agil* " " "
 ___ *bilmāla* " " "
 ___ *'addīl/gadī* Go straight!
 ___ *'aširhum bīhum* Go buy them!
 ___ *lajannam* Go to hell!
 ___ *nām, nūmi, nūmu, nūman* Go to bed!
 ___ *ṭuwāli 'isrāy* Go left!
 ___ *ṭuwāli zzēnāy* Go right!

amlis, malsa, (pl.) *mulus* smooth

amm (pl.) *-ahāt* mother
 ___ *alharrá* foster mother
 ___ *bikirīye* woman who just gave birth to her first child
 ___ *marāra* kind of stomach ailment
 ___ *miqerīfe* kind of poisonous snake

a/imm, (pls.) *umumme* ~ *amām* paternal uncle
 ___ *-a, -āt* paternal aunt

am(m) birxēn (sg./pl.) vulture

amma but, however

ammar, bi'ammir point; cause to settle an area or build a town

ammu qubiye malaria

amniyōro (no pl.) firefly

amrijēle kind of dance for girls

amsa, bimsa become night

amsaddag, bimsaddig (*b-*) sanction

amsubbāx kind of animal

amšibegāt kind of snake

amšinēne kind of tree in water

amtabaj alcoholic beverage, local brew or beer [terms used by drinkers]

amūd, (pl.) *amāyid* long stick for pounding grain
 ___ *albēt* stick for holding up a roof

amur (no pl.) command; problem

āmur ley Forgive me!

amyān, -a, -īn, -āt blind

ana I
 ___ *alla alla badōr bašīfa* I am very anxious to see him.
 ___ *bahājti badōr ley naira tinēn addōra di* I need two naira this week.
 ___ *(barjāk) fi kāno sarti (sāit/yōm) 'inta jīt* I will be in Kano until you are supposed to come.
 ___ *(barjāk) fi kāno se kan jīt* I will be in Kano until you come.
 ___ *bas fāyt al'īyāl fi āji* I am the smartest one in my class.
 ___ *dahāba mašēt lamakka* I've recently been to Mecca.
 ___ *dahābi šift alwalda* I just saw this boy.
 ___ *dāyix* I feel faint.
 ___ *farān bēk* I am happy with you.
 ___ *fāṭir* I ate breakfast/I ate during Ramadan.
 ___ *fi anjumma* I'm on vacation.
 ___ *fi llīf* " " "
 ___ *gadé ma basawwi* I never do it!
 ___ *hādi* I myself
 ___ *hāmid lēk, hāmde, -īn, -āt* I thank you.
 ___ *hāss bajildi* I feel faint.
 ___ *(illal)'āfi* ~ *āfa ley* I'm fine.
 ___ *'arfa šinu albukūn/albēsal* I know what will happen.
 ___ *'indi 'īšet rāsi* I have enough to make a living.

___ *kān farhān* I was happy.
___ *karabōni* I was staying.
___ *labudda bamši* ~ *bamši labudda* I will definitely go.
___ *ma ʾindi fendi* ~ *ma ligīt assāʾa* I am not lucky.
___ *māni* ~ *mu/i nasī(h)* I'm not well.
___ *ma/māni nigdar nimši dugut* I cannot go now.
___ *māši ke* I'm going out.
___ *mi ʾindi dāma banši lakūzīk* I don't have the chance to go to your house.
___ *miraǰǰi waṣalāna* I waited for his arrival.
___ *murr ley* I'm sad.
___ *murri mā fi* I don't care.
___ *qassátt batarbiye* I believe in education.
___ *raḍyān/rāḍi, -a, -īn, -āt* I agree.
___ *ramdān* My eyes hurt me.
___ *rāsi biwōǰīni* I have a headache.
___ *saddagta* I believe you.
___ *sawwēt širi* I'm ready.
___ *waha/īdi* I('m) alone
___ *wahmān(a) ankūn bākul naira ʾalf* I feel perhaps that I will win ₦1000.
___ *xarbān fi lmāl* I don't have any/enough money.
___ *zaʾalān fōgak* I am angry with you.

anasa evening conversation

an(a)sēt/amsēt ʾāfi, -i, -u, -an Good evening!

ančabaṭ, binčabiṭ fade, (intr.)

ančilīli (no pl.) duck (zool.)

andarabá, (coll.) *andarāb* kind of tree in bush

andarag, bindarig disappear

andardūm fist

andass (*dāxil*) Come in!

andassa, bindassa enter

andīye father's wife

andyōro (no pl.) circle

anḍaf better, best, nicer, nicest, more beautiful, most beautiful

anfarag, binfarig be divided

anfasax, binfasix peel off (intr.)

angaǰakāyá, (coll.) *angaǰak* clay bowl

angala Angala (town next to Gambaru in N.E. Nigeria)

angalab, bingalib come back, return, be returned

angálgala (small) nuts

angallo unripened fruit of the desert date palm

angāma, -āt cat

anganāgin kind of grass, growing in water, used for making mats

angara, bingari cease, stop, avoid

angara, (pl.) *anāgir* nape

angarēb (sg./pl.) small wooden bed

angarī, angári, angáru, angáran ~ *angariyán* Stop it!

angarkme copper

angātu kind of large tree in bush, used for building houses or canoes

angaṭa, bingaṭi melt

anguggum (no pl.) owl

angul, -i, -u, -an Bring!

angumāǰi, -yāt short gown, dress

angurasá, (coll.) *angurāsa* kind of small black ant

angurrmudīye, (coll.) *angurrmudu* bedbug

angūru Anguru (town in N.E. Nigeria)

angurūfu, angurūfīye, angarafa, angurūfīyāt bastard

angurūtu (sg./pl.) hippopotamus

angus ley Reduce it (the price) for me!

angušāšá, (pl.) *-āt* broom

anguši kind of gown

anhalla, binhalla be untied

anhana, binhani bend down, crouch

anhasaba chicken pox, measles
___ *karabat* + pron. suff. have or catch chicken pox or measles

anhazza, binhazza wag (intr.)

anʾadal, binʾadil stand (erect)

an'araf, bin'arif know

anīna we
___ *ahlā lēna mā lehinēn* We are enjoying that place more than this place.
___ *bayya alwālēna fi yarwa* We met each other in Maiduguri.
___ *bayya mašēna lassūk* We went together to the market.
___ *hassa rāsna 'anfata* We are civilized now.
___ *kulluna benukāna* All of us are married.
___ *ligīna rāsna* We became free (liberated).
___ *milharbīn* We are adversaries.
___ *miraǰǰi 'innak* We are waiting for you.
___ *nihawwit fi lfēḍ* We are fishing in the water.
___ *šifnā hu bas kalkal* We've seen it exactly.
___ *tābānīn funnāku* We are more tired than you.

anǰaddēna (no pl.) kind of black snake

anǰafara kind of tree or fruit thereof.

anǰamma, binǰamma relax (tr.), make s.o. rest
___ *barra* relax (intr.), be at rest
___ *šiya* Wait a bit! Take it easy!

anǰarra, binǰarra crawl along

anǰuluṭu meatless soup

anǰumma vacation, holiday

ankabūt (no pl.) spider

ankaff (sg./pl.) blow, hit

ankakor kind of orange fish

ankalaf, binkalif mature, reach puberty

ankasa, binkasi get dressed

ankasar, binkasir be broken

ankasare kind of gruel made of millet, water, milk and sugar

ankidēbise kind of tree in bush

ankučukīye, (coll.) *ánkučuk* kind of bird (larger than chicken)

ankūn maybe, perhaps

ankūru kind of dark brown fish

ankutkut whooping cough
___ *mi'ādi* contagious, infectious

annādam, binnādam repent

annaddam, binnaddam regret

annafax, binnafix swell up

annaffas, binnaffas breathe

annāhaǰ, binnāhaǰ breathe heavily

annahār ~ *annaharda* today

annaqam, binnaqam speak

annār, ___ *akalat alhille* The fire consumed the village.
___ *allahad* Sunday
___ *gammat* The fire broke out.
___ *mu/i'ōgde* The fire is lit.

annās čat all the people

annāwaṭ, binnāwaṭ reach for

anni me
___ *daraǰa* Respect me!
___ *'alme balāda* Give me more water!
(___) *ǰāy* Bring it to me here!
___ *kobo xamsa balāda* Give me another five kobo!
___ *sile balādi* Give me another shilling!

anni'ille hinē danko rubber shoes

annuǰūm kōmāt There are many stars.

ansalab, binsalib molt

ansalax, binsalix be skinned

ansarag, binsarig be stolen

ansarra, binsarra be delighted or happy

an/ššān (for) the purpose (of), in order to

anšarab, binšarib be drunk, consumed (by)

ā̃ntā̃ ~ *yā̃ntā̃* when (conj.), until

antaka, bintaki (*fōg*) lean (against)

antalaf, bintalif spoil (intr.)

antarfaká, (coll.) *antárfaka* kind of red or black insect; worm

antāri ana mā mašēt I remembered I didn't go.

antarra, bintarra move away

antāt belonging to, owned by, (for) the purpose (of)

anṭabag, binṭabig be folded, bend (intr.)

(an)ṭa(b)bāgá, -āt button

anṭaqa, -āt sandal

anṭarra, binṭarra stand in line

anṭawa, binṭawi roll up (intr.)

anṭīni ley sarti Give me a chance!

anu/im south

anxara, binxari be frightened or terrified

aqabaš tall dark grey

aq(a)laf, qalfa, (pl.) *quluf* stupid, born loser, person who never does anything right

arabi, arabīye, arab, arab(īyāt) Arab(ic)

arabīyá, -āt car, truck, lorry

arad ~ *irid, bērid* escape, run (away)

arād, birīd be interested in

āraǰ, ārǰa, (pl.) *uruǰ* lame

arak kind of tree used for making chewing sticks

arak, bērik (ēne) rub (one's eyes)

arba'a four
 ___-*'alif* four thousand

arba'īn forty

arbat, bi'arbat be spotted, have many colors

ardēbé, (coll.) *ardēb,* (pl.) *arādīb* tamarind

arḍ (m./f.) earth, land

arḍá, (coll.) *arḍa* termite, white ant

arētak bilmōt May you die!

arfa larger
 ___ *hissak* Speak louder!

arīḍ, -e, -īn, -āt wide

ārif addunya civilized person

arim, armi, -u, -an Throw!

aritak/orētak āfi I hope you are well.

arīṭ, -e, -īn, -āt heir, inheritor

arǰa, ___ *lbēt* Return home!
 ___ *šiya (ke)* Wait a bit!

arǰāni Wait for me!

arnabá, (pl.) *arnab* rabbit, hare

arra, bi'err undress

arrabbaṭ, birrabbaṭ gird oneself with cloth

arrad, bi'arrid run
 ___, *bi'arrid* ~ *bi'erred (l-)* escape, run away

arraf, bi'arrif teach
 ___ *(l-* or *b-)* introduce

arrāǰil algarn fi rāsa master drummer

arrakkas, birrakkis (fōg) depend (on)

arras, bi'arris have sexual intercourse with, sleep with, get married

arrāyad, birrāyad hate one another

arrāyib cheese

arriǰāl čat badugūnum ~ *arriǰāl čat 'indum dugunne* All men have beards.

arsal, bi'arsi/al send

arūs, (pl.) *arāyis* bride, groom

aryān, -a, -īn, -āt naked

asa width

asā̆ (f.), (pl.) *isē* (walking) stick, cane
 ___ *qalīde* big stick
 ___ *-ti* my stick

asabá, (coll.) *asab* muscle, nerve

asabettu 'āfi Good morning!

asad, (pl.) *usūd* lion

asalá, (coll.) *asal* python

āsan better, best, nicer, nicest

asar, be'esar force
 ___, *be'isir* ~ *bēsir* squeeze, rub

asarra, bisarra relax (intr.), be at rest

āsēt, -āt small tin plate

āsi, -ye, āsīn, -āt dangerous, negative (person), rebel

āsīye rebellion

askar (sg./pl.) soldier

askut Be quiet!

asma more beautiful, better, best, nicer, nicest

asqar smaller

assabb Saturday

assad, bi'assid (fōg ~ bēn) agree on

assahī truth

assājal, bissājal run quickly

assal ~ qassal, bi'/qassil wash (tr.)

as(s)al ~ is(s)al honey

assalām 'alēk(um) (traditional Muslim greeting)

assālam, bissālam greet one another

assana, ___ *ajjubā'a gāsi* This year taxes are very high.
___ *(di)* this year
___ *'attiji/jjāye/ljay* next year
___ *lfātit* last year

assaqāt, bissiqīt become angry

assar, bi'assir force, hold down

assebīti hospital

assiyāsa politics

assūdān the Sudan

assu'ul da murr bilēn sawwāni 'ana bakēt This is very sad and it made me cry.

assukkur sugar (also nickname for child)

asta'abanna, bista'abanna make fun of, mock, ridicule

aṣal, (pl.) *uṣūl* origin

aṣfar, ṣafra, (pl.) *ṣifir* yellow

aṣṣalā fard Prayer is an obligation.

aṣṣannaṭ, biṣṣannaṭ listen
___, *-i, -u, -an* Pause! Wait!

āš, bi'īš make a living

aša dinner

ašama hope (n.)

ašān šinu why (interr.)

ašana (sg./coll.) match(stick)

ašara ten
___ *(haw) arba'a* fourteen
___ ___ *itinēn* twelve
___ ___ *talāta* thirteen
___ ___ *wāhid* eleven
___ *saba* seventeen
___ *sitte* sixteen
___ *tamāni* eighteen
___ *tis'e* nineteen
___ *uxamsa* fifteen

ašgar, šagra, (pl.) *šugur* grey, light orange

ašīr (no pl.) secret, private

āšir, -e, -īn, -āt tenth

ašiya min more than (elative)

ašrak, bi'ašrik ~ bišrak talk, rebel or go against (one's religion)

ašša ~ ayyā What a pity!

aššaḍara ḍīke mugābile bēti That tree is opposite my house.

aššahar, ___ *albiji* next month
___ *halla/bihill 'amis* The new moon came out yesterday.

a/iššahi tea
māsax The tea is unsugared.

aššam the sun
___ *tifirr addini yōm* The sun rises every day.
___ *wagāt* The sun set.
___ *xanagōha* The sun eclipsed.

aš/nšān (for) the purpose (of), in order to

aššān ~ aṭišān, -a, -īn, -āt thirsty

aššar, bi'aššir signal (v.)

aššarīye law

aššāwar, biššāwar trick (v.)

(aššey) al- what (rel.)

aššīye tomorrow night

atawaffa, bitawaffa pass away, expire, die

atawwag, bitawwig look after, watch

atbāni Follow me!

atīm, -e, (pl.) *atāma* orphan

atta be accustomed to, used to (past only)

attābi nnādum alkabīr assistant manager

attafag, bittafig agree with one another

attāfax, bittāfax be a friend, be(come) friendly with, make peace

attahanna, bittahanna long or yearn for

attākal, bittākal be eaten

attālal, bittālal play at night

attalāta Tuesday

attallaf, bittallaf spoil (intr.)

attāri so
 ____ *ma ǰīt bamāl* So I didn't bring any money.

attarra, bittarra belch, burp, spit up food (for babies)

attarta, bittarta (fōg) stumble (on)

attāwab, bittāwab yawn

attāwag, bittāwag look at or after, watch

attāwak, bittāwak check (v.)

attikit ticket (for admission)

attōm, ____ *al'awwal* third month (of Islamic lunar calendar)
 ____ *arrābi* sixth month
 ____ *attālit* fifth month
 ____ *attāni* fourth month

āṭ ~ eṭa, bi'īṭ shriek, cry

aṭa, biṭī, ____ *fāga (l-)* allow s.o.
 ____ *ǰuwāb* answer (v.)

aṭ(a)rag, ṭarga, (pl.) *ṭurug* clumsy, stupid

aṭimaš, ṭamša, ṭummāš, ṭamšāt quick-tempered

aṭ(ī)ni ~ anni Give me!
 ____ *ley sarti* Give me a chance!

aṭišān ~ aššān, -a, -īn, -āt thirsty

aṭṭa addābá, biṭṭi addābá cut a diamond

aṭṭarašān (no pl.) good scent, perfume

aṭṭawāl, biṭṭāwil stretch

aṭṭawīl tallest

aṭwal min taller than

aṭyān, -īn gift
 ____ *sākit* free gift, gratuity

awa, bē'a make noise
 ____ *(b-)* complain, shout, get mad, bitch (about)

awa noise

awaǰ, bēwiǰ ~ bi'ewǰa bend (tr.)
 ____, *-āt* curve (n.)

awān when (conj.)
 ____ *da* at that time

āwan, bi'āwu/in help

āwar, -e, -īn, -āt troublemaker

āwar, ōra, awranīn, ōrānāt, (comm. pl.) *uwur* one-eyed

awīš hay

awwag, bi'awōg ~ bi'awwig injure

awwal (m./f.) formerly, first, before, previously
 ____, *-īye, -īn, -īyāt* first (ordinal)

awwalāni primary, first

awwaltāmis day before yesterday

axad, biyāxud receive
 ____ *(min)* extort (from); get married
 ____ *tār(a) fōg* take vengeance on

axaḏar, xaḏera, (pl.) *xuḏur* green, blue, black; unripe; not dry

āxar (m./f.), *āxra, lāxirīn, lāxirāt* (an)other, more, else, later, last

axašan, xašana, xašanīn, -āt, (comm. pl.) *xušun* coarse, rough, abrasive, abusive, ill-mannered

axátt tāri fōga I took vengeance on him.

axaṭṭa, buxuṭṭ beat, hit

axēr better, best, nicer, nicest
 ____ *ǰa kān mi ke su'ul wāhid bukūn* He should come or else something bad will happen.

axīde, (pl.) *axāyid* wedding, marriage

axti haw ʾaxuy ma birrāyadu ~ *axti haw ʾaxuy ma birūdu gabīla* My sister and brother hate each other.

axu, (pls.) *ixwān* ~ *ayay/wān* brother
 ___ *magaǰi* eldest brother
 ___ *-t,* (pl.) *axawāt* sister

axx Alas! Woe!

axxar, bi ʾaxxir postpone, come or make late

ay so ʾol everything

aya, ayi, ayō, ayan Be tired!

āya, -āt verse of Koran

ayab/ya banana

ayʾ yes

āyib(āy), āybe, -īn, -āt wicked

āyim, āyme, -īn, -āt swimming

ayya, bi ʾeyyi make s.o. tired

ayyā ~ *aššа* What a pity!

ayyad, bi ʾayyid help

ayya(ʾ) mom(my)

ayyan, bi ʾayyin search or look for; make s.o. very tired or angry

ayyān, -a, -īn, -āt very tired, exhausted

ayyar, bi ʾeyyir abuse, insult, curse

ayyas, bi ʾayyis despair, lose hope

ayyaṭ, bi ʾayyiṭ make s.o. shout out

ayyi any

ayyōm wallambākir sooner or later

ayyōm(da) today
 ___ *dugō mašēt* ~ ___ *hatta ma mašēt* I didn't go until today.

ayyut every
 ___ *sabāh* every morning
 ___ *subū* every morning

āza, bi ʾāzi console, extend sympathy

azab, (pl.) *uzubān* bachelor, widower
 ___ *-á, -āt* divorce, widow, harlot, unmarried girl (not a virgin)

āzab, bi ʾāzib torture

azal, bi ʾizil elect

azalīye accident

azam, bēzam decide

azik Azik (p.n.m.)

azīm, -e, (pl.) *uzām* grand, outstanding

azōxar, bizēxar move

azrag, zarga, (pl.) *zurug* black (person)
 ___ *čil/kurum* very black, pitch black

azumá, -āt ceremony, celebration
 (___*hīl*) *anǰumma* holiday, vacation

azyan better

azzabūra Bible

azzal, bi ʾezzil choose

azzam, bi ʾazzim invite

azzamān nowadays

azzēn better, best, nicer, nicest

azzeyyen, bizēn shave

B

b- in, to, with

ba- have, possess

ba warā straight backwards

bāb (*albēt*), (pl.) *bībān* (*albēt*) door

baba rīga big gown

bāba dad(dy)

bābar, bibābar threaten

babī'a ha I won't sell it.

bābūr, -āt motorcycle

bada, bibda/i start, begin (to do s.t.)

badal change (money) (n.)
 ____, *bubdul* change money (v.)

baddad, bibaddid spill (tr./intr.)
 ____ (*addamm*) shed (blood)

baddal, bibaddil exchange, change (money)

baddiwāy, (pl.) *badu* Bedouin, nomad

badīn, -e, -īn, -āt wealthy; incorrigible

badōr tīlas timíš lazāria 'ambākir I insist you go to Zaria tomorrow.

bāḍa, bibīḍ lay an egg

bafā'aila terrible

bafdu (no pl.) sickle, scythe

bāgá, -yāt shock (of corn)

bagará, (coll.) *bagar* cow, bovine, (coll.) cattle

bagas, bubgus reduce (price)

bagga, bubugg (*min*) leave

baggāri, (pl.) *baggārīn* cattleman

baggas, bibaggis reduce (price)

bāgi remainder, rest; ago
 ____ *dōrtēn* two weeks ago
 ____ *sā'a wāhid/wāhade* one hour ago
 ____ *san(a)tēn* two years ago
 ____ *yōmēn* two days ago

bāgud bākul I will begin to eat.

bagudra by or with force, forcefully

bahāǰa + pron. suff. + *dār* need (v.)

bahar ~ *bihir,* (pls.) *buhūr* ~ *buhurre* lake, river

bahīme, (pl.) *bahā'/yim* animal

bā'a, bibī'a [village use:] sell; [city use:] buy

ba'ad after
 ____ *adduhur* in the afternoon (generally after two o'clock)

ba('a)dēn later on, afterwards

ba'ar ~ *bār* dirty, manure, feces, dung

ba'ašōm ~ *bāšom,* (pls.) *ba'āšīm* ~ *bāšim* jackal

ba'īd, -e, -īn, -āt far, distant

ba'ōḍa ~ *ba'udá* ~ *bawda,* (coll.) *ba'ūd* mosquito

bāǰa ~ *čāga* pelican

baka, bibki ~ *bubukk* cry, moo, mew

bakān algrā (no pl.) school

bakī cry(ing) (n.)

bakkar, bibakkir go early in the morning; have one's first child

baktar, (pl.) *bakātir* leather bag for books, cover of the Koran

(*bal*)*'aǰala* fast, quickly

bāl concern, opinion; body of water without vegetation

bāl, bubūl urinate

b/walā without
 ____ *fāyde/fāydāt/manfa'a/manāfi* useless
 ____ *rā'i* by or with force, forcefully
 ____ *rās/yaqīn* at random

___ *sā'a* unfortunate
___ *šakk* doubtless
___ *taman* free (of charge), gratis

balad, (pl.) *bilād* town, province, place

balād + pron. suff. another, more

balāk, -i, -u, -an negation (2nd person pres.)
—— *-i 'ārife* You (f.sg.) don't know.

bālam I dream.

balas, bubulus lose (tr.)

(bal)bišēš careful(ly), slow(ly)

balgū by or with force, forcefully

balhēl quickly, fast(er), forceful(ly), loud(ly)

bal'agil slow(ly)

balīle boiled guinea corn

bālix, bālqe, -īn, -āt rude

balla, bibill make wet

balmarkaba by ship

balyān, -a, -īn, -āt weak

balyaqīn for sure

bāmā' Bama (Arabic-speaking town in N.E. Nigeria, 45 miles southeast of Fort-Lamy)

bambar, -āt bed

bambūsá, (coll.) *bambūs* pawpaw (bot.)

banān nās person of well-to-do family (f.pl.)

bandala celebrating dance for men (especially during harvest time)

bandāma, (pl.) *-yīn* fisherman

bandar, (pl.) *banādir* capital city

bandirá, (coll.) *bandar* wild crop

bango wall (of a small round hut)

bani building, construction

bank(i), (pl.) *bankiyāt* bank (financial)

ban(n)a, bibinn build

bannāy, -īn builder

banūn, -a, -īn, -āt sweet-smelling

banyān building (gerund)

baqaḏ, bubquḏ hate

bāqas, bibāqis make s.o. angry

baqīd, -e, -īn, -āt enemy

barad ice, hail
___, *buburud* cool off, not make any trouble

baradi ~ *b(a)rōdi* ~ *brēdi* bread

barak, bubruk kneel down, praise; light up
___ *-atak* Greetings!

bārak, bibārak bless

baram, bub(u)rum turn upside down, screw

baras white leprosy

bardā' coolness

bardān, -a, -īn, -āt cold (anim.)

bardāya ~ *albardā'* cold season

bardūl, (pl.) *barādīl* long, sharp knife

bargōyá, (pls.) *barāgo* ~ *bargwayāt* blanket

barī innocent, not guilty

bārid, bārde, -īn, -āt cool

bārikalḻa ~ *barakalḻa* Praise be to God!

barka good fortune
___ *ba'alḻa ǰābak bal'āfi* God bless you and bring you health!
___ *baǰīt bal'āfi* Greetings!
___ *lēk* Congratulations!

barkan, bibarkin be rusty

barkān rust (n.)

barnak (no pl.) garbage, rubbish

barra outside
___ *min alhille* out of town

barrad, bibarrid bathe or wash s.o./oneself

barrād, -āt teapot

barrāg lightning

barūd bath

bas only

bas/talá, (coll.) *bas/tal* onion

basam, bibsim smile

basaṭ, bubsuṭ welcome

baskur bicycle

basma (no pl.) smile

baṣāra cleverness, discreetness

baṣīr, -e, -īn, -āt clever, discreet

bāš salary, wages

bašīme stillborn child

baššar, bibaššir bring good news

batar, bubtur loosen

bātir battery

bat(t)ān after that, again

bātu after

baṭālá, -āt holiday, vacation

bāṭalān, -a, -īn, -āt thin

bāṭil, -e, -īn, -āt thin

baṭin stomach, womb, uterus; course
____ *mankarbe* be constipated
____ *-a mankarbe* He is constipated.

baṭīr I fly.

baṭirān, -a, -īn, -āt troublemaker

baṭṭān (sg./pl.) rope for tying a load on donkey

baṭṭayāra by plane

bawaǰā pain

bawda ~ *ba'ōḍa* ~ *ba'udá*, (coll.) *ba'ūd* mosquito

bawre kind of tree

baxat richness, luck

baxīt, -e, -īn ~ *buxāt, -āt* rich, wealthy (man)

baxīt Baxit (p.n.m.)
____ *-e* Baxite (p.n.f.)

baxxar, bibaxxir smoke (of perfume)

bayāḍ reward (n.)

bāyaḍ, bibāyiḍ reward (v.)

bāyin, bāyne, -īn, -āt evident, clear, apparent

bāyir, bāyre, -īn, -āt barren (of land)

bāyre having no lover (f.)

bayyaḍ, bibayyiḍ reward

bayyan, bibayyin find s.o.

bayyin, bibayyin explain

bāz, (pl.) *bīzān* eagle

bazar, bubzur sprout, grow, mature (bot. only)

bazax, bubzux spit

bazzar, bibazzir germinate; squander money

be sale

be- + *nukā* + pron. suff. married

bēḍé, (colls.) *bēḍ/ṣ̌* egg

be/ahisāb according to

be'erif aššūm He is modest.

bel, (pl.) *bīlān* belt

bēni haw bēnak between you and me

berbere guinea corn planted after the rainy season

bēt, (pls.) *b(i/u)yūt* house, room
____ *al'axīde* marriage house
____ *alladāy* kitchen
____ *almarīse* bar, pub
____ *alwāya* post office
____ *assēf* scabbard
(____*aš*)*šarī'e* courthouse
____ *attāba* cigarette factory

bidā beginning, start

bidin, bubdan become rich

bidōr l- need (v.)

bigdar buktub He is able to write.

bigī, bibga be(come), happen, remain

bihēla, bihēlha, -um, -īn strong, powerful

bihēr, -āt creek

bi/ukar Bukar (p.n.m.)

bikēt packet

bikir, bikirīye (f.) firstborn

biladēga small village

bilāmá (*lhille*) head of small village

bil(h)ēn a lot, lots, much, very (much)

bilīle boiled guinea corn

bilmāla ~ *bilmahala* slow(ly)

bin nās person of well-to-do family (f.sg.)

bineyye, -āt daughter, little girl; baby, infant toddler (f.)

bīr (f.), (pls.) *b(i)yūr* ~ *biyār* ~ *bīrān* well (for water)

birāri, (f.) *tirāri* singer

b(i)rāya ke (all genders/numbers) nonsense, useless

birdi kind of grass in water

bi/urdugula (no pl.) big lizard

biri, bibra cover

birī, bu/ibra recover, be cured

birke, (pl.) *burūk* spring (of water)

birku white guinea corn

birmil, (pl.) *baramīl* barrel

birnāy, birnā'iye, barno, birnāyāt Kanuri person

birš, (pl.) *b(i)rūš* sleeping mat

birūǰ trumpet, bugle

bisāri kind of game (played)

bi/usāṭ, (pls.) *bisiṭṭe* ~ *-at* carpet

biskīt, (pl.) *basākīt* biscuit

bisklet, (pl.) *bisklāt* bicycle

bišāra ~ *bišir* good news

bišēš careful(ly), slow(ly)

biši, -ye, biš'īn, -āt ugly

bitt, (pl.) *banāt* daughter, girl, virgin
___ *al'axu(t)* niece
___ *almulk* (f.) of good grade or class
___ *fatā* virgin
___ *'imm* female paternal cousin
___ *walad* granddaughter
___ *xāl* female maternal cousin

bittāwab fin subbāṭ anni'ās kāribinna He will yawn because he is sleepy.

biṭṭēxé, (coll.) *biṭṭēx* (water)melon

biyāri my wells

bizāx spit (n.)

bōči Bauchi (name of city and hills in N.E. Nigeria)

bōǰa, biwōǰi(h) be in pain, hurt (intr.)

bol ball

bōl urine

bolīs police

bō/ūṭá, (pls.) *bawāṭ* ~ *buwōṭ* ~ *bawāyiṭ* ~ *bīṭān* small body of water, pond, medium-sized lake, dam

brēdi bread

buḍā (sg./pl.) goods for sale

būg, (pl.) *bawaga* round calabash; kind of local wind instrument

buhū hana lqalla sack of guinea corn

bu/akān(á), (pl.) *bikinne* place, post, position, assignment
___ *addalāl* playground
___ *azzugā* irrigated place

bukān(it) almasra grazing place

bukra occasionally, the day after tomorrow

bukūn possible; possibly, perhaps

bukuti, (pl.) *bukutyāt* bucket

būmi, būmīye, (pl.) *bawama* bastard

bundūg, (pl.) *banādīg* gun

bunni, bunnīye, -yīn, -yāt brown, coffee-colored

būrīye, (pl.) *būrāyāt* farm

burkutu alcoholic beverage, local beer (term used by drinkers)

burlālá, (pl.) *barālīl* blister

burma, (pls.) *b(i/u)rām* large pot
___ *-at allaban* milk pot
___ *-at 'alme* small olla

burūda rheumatism

busāyá, (pl.) *būs* nose ring

busxa, (pl.) *bisax* calabash pot

buxāra new grass

C

čabāt flogging (n.)

čabba, bučubb cut down, fell

čabba ke soon

čabbat, bičabbit pull out by the roots

čāča, bičāči be cunning or sly, play a trick on s.o.

čād Chad

čāga ~ *bāǰa* pelican

čāka, (pls.) *-yāt* ~ *čayayāt* loom

čakčaká, (coll.) *čakčak* kind of tall grass

čakka, bučukk ~ *bičuxx,* ___ (d.o. ~ *fi*) stab; plant; pitch (a tent); gamble
___ (*nafsa*) stick (oneself)

čakkāba, -āt fish basket

čakkat, bičakkit prepare land for plowing

čakram, bičakrim lock

čalbané, (pl.) *čálbane* fishhook

čalla, biče/alli cut trees or bushes, prune, harvest

čallā, (pl.) *-yāt* small axe

čanna, bičinn ~ *bučunn* wipe clean, paint

čat all, whole, either
___ (*ke*) all together
___ *wāhid* same, similar, equal
___ (*-ta*) *wāhid* (*ley*) It's all the same!

čēl (sg./pl.) trap (for animals)

čenǰi change (money) (n.)

čerčerīye, -āt girl of approx. 12-15 years

čilal hawk

čokoli, (pl.) *čokolyāt* kind of spoon

čukkāy, (coll.) *čukka* small bird that eats guinea corn and insects

čurūru salt made from millet

Ḍ

ḍahar, (pls.) ḍuhūr ~ ḍuhurre back (anat.)

ḍa(ha)wīye, (coll.) ḍahāwe cloud
 ____ bilēn It's cloudy./Soon it will rain.

ḍalām, (pl.) ḍulūm darkness

ḍalla (no pl.) monkey
 ____ l'axaḍar/l'azrag (no pls.) baboon

ḍalma, (pl.) ḍulūm dark place

ḍamāna liability, security

ḍam(b) fōg responsible for

ḍamīn, -e, -īn, -āt guardian

ḍāmin, -a, -īn, -āt lender, guarantor

ḍ/zam(m), (pls.) ḍ/zunūb responsibility, sin

ḍān (f.), (d.) -ēn, (pls.) dunne ~ ḍinne ear

ḍarīr, -a, -īn, -āt jealous of s.o.

ḍarra across, opposite, facing; antonym

ḍarra, (pls.) -āt, ~ ḍarāyir co-wife

ḍarra, biḍirr cheat, swindle

ḍarrāba pepper-like fruit

ḍarūra cheating (n.)

ḍawwa, biḍawwi shine, (of the sun)

ḍayya, biḍaww/yyi illuminate

ḍayyaf, biḍayyif offer hospitality

ḍēf, (pls.) ḍīfān ~ ḍyūf (addār) stranger, foreigner (from out of town), guest

ḍe/ay(y) light (n.)
 ____ algamar moonlight
 ____ʾannahār daylight
 ____ aššam sunlight

ḍīfe act of being a guest

Ḏ̣

ḏ̣āk(a) (m.), ḏ̣īke (f.) that (pron.), (over) there

ḏ̣ēlāka these

ḏ̣ōlā/-ōka (m.), ḏ̣ēlaka (f.) those (farther away)

D

dā̃ (m.), *di* (f.) this
  ____ *alla l'arāda* This is God's wish!
  ____ *arrakkas fōg aššurūṭ* That depends.
  ____ *ba'īd min alyaqīn* This is improbable.
  ____ *balā bikān* This is impossible.
  ____ *bāy'inna* This is sold.
  ____ *bukūn* This is possible.
  ____ *fāyit ḍāka* This is better.
  ____ *haggi* This is mine.
  ____ *hana be* This is for sale.
  ____ *haqīqa* This is true.
  ____ *hayyin ana 'arfinna* This is simple; I know it.
  ____ *hu* Here it is.
  ____ *'ēb lēk/fōgak* Shame on you!
  ____ *'ēbak 'inta* You are guilty.
  ____ *kalkal* This is exactly so.
  ____ *katīr* That's a lot.
  ____ *ke* This is so.
  ____ *kōma* This is a lot/too much.
  ____ *kuč* That's all right.
  ____ *lbigī* ~ ____ *l'amr albigī* This is what happened.
  ____ *ma bibga* This is impossible.
  ____ *mā bukūn* This is impossible.
  ____ *mi bālak* It's none of your concern.
  ____ *mi hāǰti* It's none of my business.
  ____ *mi ke* This isn't so.
  ____ *murr* This is sad.
  ____ *qadar alla* ~ ____ *alla alqaddara* This is God's will.
  ____ *su'ul aššurūṭ asawanna* It all depends.

dābá, (pl.) *dahab* diamond

dabah, budbah slaughter

dabangá, (pl.) *dabang* bin made of mud for storing guinea corn

dabāra (no pl.) plan

dabārá, -āt trick (n.)

dabaz, budbuz beat, hit, hammer

dabba, -āt hill, mound

dabba, bidibb creep

dabbā('), (pl.) *dabbāyāt* large waterskin used to pull up well water

dabbar, bidabbir change one's mind

dabbāyá, -āt water bucket

dabbāza, -āt hammer

dabdab, bidabdib pat, level (a road)

dabi ~ *dabībe*, (pl.) *dabīb* worm, snake

dabīhe, -āt celebration

d/ǰabīr, -e, -īn, -āt wise, clever, hard-working

dafa cheek

dafak, bud(u)fuk go (away), leave

dafan, bud(u)fun bury

dafar, budufur weave
  ____ *albirš* make a mat

daffa, bidaffi boil, cook (tr.), prepare food
  ____, *buduff* push, shove

daffa/daft-, (pls.) *-āt* ~ *dufūf* house, place; side, on the other side of, next to

daffak, bidaffik spill (tr.)

daft/dar, (pls.) *dafāt/dir* notebook

dāg, bidūg taste
  ____, *budūg* become narrow

dagalé, (pl.) *daggāli* big calabash

dagalí, (pl.) *dagāli* clay bed

dagas, bud(u)gus be ill
  ____ *šie ke* He was a little ill.

dagaš, buduguš run (to), collide, knock down

dagdāgá thunder

dagga, budugg hit, beat, pound, hammer; spank; grind

—— *allōda* ring a bell, beep a horn

daggāg alb(i/u)rām, (pl.) *-īn alb(i/u)rām* potter

dagīg, -e, (pl.) *dugāg* small, minute, young; flour, meal, powder, coarsely-ground guinea corn
___ *algahawa* powdered coffee

dagīg(a), (d.) *dagīgēn,* (pls.) *dagāy/'ig* minute
___ *talāta* ~ *dagāyig talāta* three minutes

dagōyá, -āt black mat (for sitting or decoration)

dahā 8:00 to 10:00 A.M.
___ *lqanam* 8:00 to 9:00 A.M.

dahab gold

dahabá, (coll.) *dahāb* dark cloud

dahāba/i recently, just, yet
___ *ǰā* He has just come.
___ *ǰīt* I have just come.
___ *māši/bimši* He is just going.

da/ehadda ~ *(da)hādi* exactly, then, all right, (and) so, quite so, just so

dahakāt front teeth

dahalōb, (pl.) *dahālīb* clay lid

d/tahar, bit(h)ar ~ *bittar* stop (tr.)

dahará sandy earth or ground

dahhar, bithar warn

da/ihīye, (coll.) *dahí* egg

da'awa, -āt complaint

dakar, (pl.) *dukūr* male, masculine

dakko lēya walad There is a boy.

dala, budla be lame

dālal, bidālal play an instrument

dalamāyá, (pl.) *dalam* kind of gourd used for gruel, food or water

dāle, dāle, dālīn, -āt weak

dāli, -ye, dālīn, -āt lame

dalla (no pl.) slope
___, *bidalli* slope down, go down a slope, land, dismount, unload
___, *bidalla (falṭa)* climb (down)

dallālá, -āt umbrella

dallāti, -ak, dallākki, -a, dallāytaha, dallāyna, dallāyikku, dallāyikkan, dallāyithum, dallāyithin then (at that time)

dalomma humma (m.), *dēlenna hinna* (f.) Here they are.

dalū, (pls.) *dalawa* ~ *dalwāt* water bucket (usually made of leather)

dalūl, -a, -īn, -āt docile, pacifist(ic)

dama, (pl.) *dumū* tear (from the eye)

damā', budma weep

dāma chance, opportunity
___, *bidāmi (fi)* bother, interfere with

damāná witness

damm blood

damm, budumm keep, preserve

damm ke so that

damma, budumm collect, put away

dāna, bidāni come near, approach

danab, (pl.) *dunūb* tail

dandal, (pl.) *danādil* playground, place in which talking and playing occur at night; palace

dangá drum

dangá, (d.) *dangatēn,* (pl.) *dawange* jail, prison cell

dangar, bidangar put down, lower; bend down, crouch

dāni, -ye, -yīn, -yāt near

danǰa, -āt turnsignal (of a car)

dankāli (no pl.) sweet potato
___ *-t annaṣ̈āra* potato

dankikīye, -āt kind of sleeveless shirt

danko rubber

danni maybe, perhaps

daqay, -e, -īn, -āt troublemaker

dar small ant

dār, bidīr vomit

____, *bidōr* want
____, ____ (*tīlas*) insist
____, *budūr* encircle, surround
____, (f.), (pl.) *dīrān* (nomad) camp
____, *sayyārīn* camp with cattle and horses
____ (f.), (pls.) *d(u)yūr* ~ *diyār* land, country(side), place, area, territory; town
____ *alqurūb/alqurba* foreign country

dara, bidirr (*fōg*) put on
____, *bidri* know

darab, budrub hit, strike, beat
____ *allōda* ring a bell, beep a horn
____ *ankaff* strike s.o. with a blow
____ *fi nnuggāra* beat a drum
____ *ʾagil* disturb, confuse

daraǰa respect (n.)

darangal ~ *dringil,* (pl.) *darangīl* wooden bed tied with leather

daras, budrus read, study
____ *fi galba* memorize
____ *-i* subject, topic

daraš, budruš grind up coarsely

darat harvest time (Nov.-Dec.)

darb, (pl.) *durūb* path(way), road, street [village use]
____ *albēt* door
____ *alǰirgi* railroad track
____ *alwatīl* highway

darbá, -āt lash(ing), flogging

dardam, bidardim make s.t. round or into a ball

darēt muxultí fōg kitifí I put my bag on my shoulder.

dargas, bidargis roll (down) (tr.)

darkubá, -āt small cart

darrābá axadar green vegetable

darraǰ, bidarriǰ (make s.o.) go slowly

darras, bidarris teach

dars, (pl.) *durūs* molar

dass alxumām dāxil He put the things inside.

dassa, bidiss put on or inside

____ *b/walā ʾizin algumnati* smuggle
____ *ʾīda* sign (one's name)

dassāku fīni šinu What's bothering you?

dassēt sōsōʾi fi riǰilí I put on my socks.

dātēn early, on time, now

dawa just (adv.)
____ (*lēya*) *aššahi hinēn* There is tea here.

dawā' (no pl.) medicine
____ *sabīb* laxative

dāwa ink

dāwa, bidāwi cure with medicine

dāwam, bidāwam endure

dāwas, bidāwis fight

dāwax, bidāwix make s.o. faint

dawāyá, -āt inkwell

dawdi curved sword

dawwa anyhow

daw(w)a almāl da Here is the money.

daw(w)a lēya hu ǰāy Here he is coming.

daw(w)ar, bidawwir want
____ + impf. be going to or about to
____ (*l-*) find

dawwas, bidawwis fight

dawwās(i), -a, -īn, -āt fighter, pugnacious person

dawwir alxēl Get the horses!

dāx, bidūx faint

daxal, buduxul enter
____ *-a* entrance

dāxil inside

daxxal, bidaxxil put inside, make s.o. enter

daxxan, bidaxxin smoke or have a cigarette

dāyik, dāyke, -īn, -āt laughing

dāyir, dāyre, -īn, -āt round

dāyman always

dāyre, -āt wheel

dayyag, bidayyig worry (tr.)

dayyan, bidayyin (l-) lend (money)

dayyāni, (pl.) *dayyānīn* creditor

dayyig, dayyge, -īn, -āt narrow

dēd, (pl.) *d(i)yūd* breast, tit, teat

dehdda (and) then

dēl(a) these

delēbé, (coll.) *delēb* kind of tree

dēlenna hinna Here they are (f.).
 ___ *albanāt* Here are these girls.

de/alīl (no pl.) reason

dēn, (pl.) *duyūn* debt

derwīš, (pl.) *darāwīš* old pious man
 ___ *-iye, -āt* old pious woman

di this (f.)
 ___ *hīli* This is mine.
 ___ *jēt al'awwal hinēn* This is the first time I've come here.
 ___ *sarti al'āxar/alwarrāni albamši lakūzīk* This is the last time I'll go to your house.

dibin, (pl.) *dabana* large pot for water or grain

digé only

digilāba, (pl.) *dagālīb* porch

digin, (pls.) *dugūn* ~ *dugunne* beard, chin
 ___ *čukūt* short beard
 ___ *dāyre* long beard
 ___ *xāzūk* man with bad manners

diglāba, (pl.) *dagālīb* marketplace hut (occasionally lived in)

dihib, bitab get lost

dihik, bitak laugh

dihītēn second month (of Islamic lunar calendar)

dihīye first month (of Islamic lunar calendar)

dihne, (coll.) *dihin* shortening, butter

dīje Didje (p.n.f.)

dīk, (pl.) *dayaka* rooster, cock, turkey

dikēči, (pl.) *dikēčīn* barber

dīko, -yīn grandson, (pl.) grandchildren

dīkwa Dikwa (town in N.E. Nigeria)

dilēl, -āt (small) shady area

dilīle, (pls.) *dalāl* ~ *dulūl* game (played)

dīn religion
 ___ *annaṣāra* Christianity

dīne ~ *dihne,* (colls.) *dīn* ~ *dihin* shortening, butter
 ___ *fūl* ~ ___ *hana kolči* groundnut oil

dirāya knowledge

dirbé, (pl.) *dirāb* tumor, cyst

dirdīme anything round

dirdir, (pl.) *darādir (albēt)* wall (of a house)

d/jīre neighborhood

dirīsa Dirisa (p.n.m.)

dīya almarabá Here is the shirt.

diyāla dubbāná hinēn There is a fly here.

diyāná, (pl.) *duyūn* borrowing, loan

diye (no pl.) blood money, ransom

dōdo evil spirit

dōgar, bidōgar (fōg) depend (on)

dogāri prison guard

doktor, (pl.) *dakātīr* doctor

dōl (m.), *dēla* (f.) those (near)
 ___ *-a 'al'īyāl* Here are those boys.

dōle must

dōm kind of large tree (such as a date palm)

dōr, (pl.) *dīrān* temporary village (during dry season)

dōrá, (d.) *dōrtēn,* (pl.) *-āt* cycle, week

dōri dried meat, jerky

dōyá, -āt yam

dringil ~ *darangal,* (pl.) *darangīl* wooden bed tied with leather

dubbāná, (coll.) *dubbān* fly

dūdá ~ *dūdāyá,* (coll.) *dūd* insect, worm
 ___ *albile* red ant
 ___ *almaṭara* rain mite (red insect during rainy season)

duffa bread

duggāg, -a, -īn, -āt tiny

duggut immediately, right now

 ___ *duggut* immediately, right now, suddenly (emphatic)

dugō before, (not) yet, until, then, nearly

dugut soon, now

 ___ *ankūn fi kāno walla (ankūn kān) fi zāria* Now maybe he is either in Kano or Zaria.

duhur afternoon (12:00 to 4:00 P.M.)

dūǰ/zi (no pl.) owl

dukāy, (no pl.) *dawaka* drummer

dukk all

dukkān, (pl.) *dakākīn* shop

dukōye, (pl.) *dukōyāt* granddaughter

dull, (pl.) *dalala* shade

dumbāyá, (pl.) *danābi* large calabash

dumbur, (pl.) *danābir* stump (bot.)

dunguso, (pl.) *danāgis* dump

dunya ~ *di/uniya* (no pl.) world, (with def. art.) future

duquš duquš predawn

durā red guinea corn

durbān, (pl.) *darābīn* big wildcat

dūri family, tribe

durūb dayygāt narrow roads

durus, (pl.) *durūs* rough-edged blade

dūt (sg./coll.) lion

duwāra, -āt small lake

duwās, -āt fight(ing)

duxān (no pl.) smoke

duxun (no pl.) millet

E

ēb, (pl.) *ībān* fault, shame
____ *aššūm* disgrace

ebid, (pls.) *a/ebīd* slave

ebrīg, (pl.) *ebārīg* jug, pitcher, kettle (usually for ablution, but also for other purposes)

efana (no pl.) bad smell

ēli youth

ēmar ~ *eʾmar* ~ *ahmar, hamra,* (pl.) *humur* red, pink
____ *ču* bright red, very red

ēn, (ds.) *ēne* ~ *ēnēn,* (pl.) *uyūn* eye
____ *qalīde* big eye

ēsar, isrāye, isrāyīn, -āt left-handed

ēš food; cooked guinea corn or millet
____ *hana lgalīsa* cassava gruel

eṭa ~ *āṭ, biʾīṭ* cry, shriek, scream, shout

ēṭá, (coll.) *ēṭ* cry, shriek, scream, shout

ēy yes

F

fačax, bifčax step on (once)

faččax, bifaččix step on (repeatedly)

fačiq stepping, treading or trampling on

fad(a)ri (no pl.) mule

faddil dāxil Come inside please!

faḍāyat, -yāt albēt courtyard

faḍḍal, bifaḍḍil leave behind; be left, remain
 ___ ~ *faddil* Please!

faḍī, -he, -hīn, -hāt person who makes others laugh

fāḍi ~ *faḍāya,* (pl.) *faḍayāt* open space

fāgá, (pl.) *-āt* chance, opportunity; vacation, holiday

fagad, bufgud rafīg lose a friend

fagāra poverty

faggūsá, (coll.) *faggūs* cucumber

fagīr, -e, -īn, -āt poor

fahala courage

faham charcoal

fahham bifahhim make understood

fāhil, -e, -īn, -āt brave person

fahīm -e, -īn, -āt very intelligent

faʾal, bifʾal do great things, fight against great odds; cause damage

faʾara wādīn some teachers (m./f.)

fājar, bifājir go early in the morning

fajir dawn, 6:00 to 8:00 A.M.

fājir, -e, -īn, -āt precocious

fajjar, bifajjir get up at dawn

fakar, bufkur be careful or thoughtful

fakī, (pl.) *fakīn* (male) teacher of Islamic subjects, usually Koran

fākir, -e, -īn, -āt careful

fakka, bufukk open (v.)

fakkar, bifakkir remind, think, ponder
 ___ (*l-*) take care of, protect
 ___, *bufkur* ~ *bifakkir* (*fi* ~ *l-*) pay attention, notice

fakkir l- Beware of . . . !

falajá (no pl.) gap between one's front teeth

fāli kind of green melon with black seeds

falla, bifill spread, unroll

fallāl, -āt harpoon

fallāti, fallatīye, fallāta (m./comm.), *fallātīyāt* Fulani

falṭa ~ *falṭāni* below, under, down (prep.), lower, on the floor/ground

falū, (pl.) *filāw* colt, foal

falwa, -āt filly

fam pound (Nigerian currency = 2 naira)

famfam water tap

fanazzāra name of a star

fangame (no pl.) spur

fange, (pl.) *fangāyāt* straw hat

fannad, bifannid separate, distinguish

fannid lēna lkalām Tell us what's going on!

fānūs, (pl.) *fawānīs* kerosene lamp

faqīr, (pls.) *faq/ʾara* ~ *fuqrān* ~ *-īn* (male) teacher of Islamic subjects, usually Koran; beggar

fār, bufūr boil (intr.)

farādá, (pls.) *-āt* ~ *farādi* saddle blanket

farag, bufrug separate

fārag, bifārig pass away, expire

faragá, -āt chance

farāha happiness

farak, buf(u)ruk hold s.t. in one's hand, screw

farān, -a, -īn, -āt happy

farārīǰ young chickens, chicks

faras, (pl.) *fursān* horse, mare

farasīya bravery

faraš, bufruš spread, beat (a carpet), punish
 ___ *albirš* Spread the carpet!

fārá(y), (coll.) *fār* mouse, rat

fard religious obligation

farḍá, (pl.) *firāḍ* clothes (women only)

farḍá, (pl.) *furūḍ* tribal marks (anywhere on one's body)

farente (sg./pl.) dish, plate, small tin or glass plate

farfoá, (coll.) *farfo* type of grey fish

farg, (pl.) *furūg* difference

farīd, -e, -īn, -āt alone

farīd seventh month (of Islamic lunar calendar)

farīk fresh guinea corn

fāris, -īn brave fighter, warrior

farmā assignment, position, post

farmalá ~ *fármala,* (pl.) *farāmil* shirt with no collar or sleeves

farr, bifirr rise

fa/urr, (pls.) *furūr* ~ *firār* tree branch

farra, bifirr ~ *bufurr* jump, pounce

farrak, bifarrik brand children 12-13 years old for tribal initiation

farrāk, -āt screwdriver

farrāšá, -āt rug, saddle blanket, bed clothes

farrāši, (pl.) *farrāšīn* peddler

farrūǰ, -īn young male chicken or rooster
 ___ *-á, -āt* young female chicken, pullet

fartak, bifartik (fōg) move around

farūṭ snakeskin

farwa, (pls.) *f(a)rāw* (human/animal) skin, leather

farx (sg./pl.) type of paper, large sheet of paper

farxitan kalt kind of fish

fās (f.), (pls.) *fawāsa* ~ *fáwasa* axe
 ___ *qalīde* large axe

fasa, bifsi break wind

fasāha, -āt explanation; eloquence, skill

fasal, bufsul cut off; be intelligent

fasax, bifsax lie, prevaricate
 ___, *bufsux* bud (of guinea corn)

fasī, -he, -hīn -hāt eloquent, skillful

fasil, -e, -īn, -āt bad, evil, wicked

fāsil, -e, -īn, -āt very intelligent

fāsix, fāsxe, -īn, -āt (comm. pl.) *fussāx* liar

fassal, bifassil show; divide

fassar, bifassir explain, translate, interpret (esp. Koran)

fassāx, -e, -īn, -āt habitual liar

fa/usux (no pl.) lie

fašar, bufšur boast

fāšir, -āt open space, courtyard
 ___, (pl.) *fawāšir* palace

faššār, -a, -īn, -āt boastful

fāt, bufūt go around, pass by, surpass

fata, bifta (l-) get married

fatagá, -āt space between parked cars

fatah, biftah open (v.)

fatal, buftul filhibāl braid rope

fāti(h), -ha, -hīn, -hāt open (adj.)

fātihe marriage prayer

fattak, bifattik unfasten

fattal, bifattil twist

fattāni, fattāna, -īn, -āt conspirator, instigator

fattaš, bifattiš look (for); discover, figure out, find s.t.

fattāš, -īn principal, visiting teacher

fatyān arrās civilization

faṭar. bu/ifṭur eat breakfast (together); eat during Ramadan

fāṭime Fatime (p.n.f.)

fāṭir, (pl.) *fawāṭir* incisor

faṭirēn twelfth month (of Islamic lunar calendar)

faṭīs (no pl.) animal that died of natural causes, carrion

faṭūr breakfast

fāwar, bifāwir boil (tr.)

fawwar, bifawwir boil (tr.)

fawwat, bifawwit (*allēl*) spend the night

fāyde, -āt use, usefulness, advantage, benefit

fāyir boiling, fire

fāyit, fāyte, -īn, -āt better, superior, more than (elative)
 ____ *al'awwalāni* more than the first time

faza help (n.)
 ____, *bifza* help s.o. in danger, save
 ____, (f.) *faza'at, bifza* (*l-*) bring or carry s.t. from the bush

fazzāy, -a, -īn, -āt helper

fēḍ flood(water), water

fende, (pl.) *fendāyāt* small- to medium-sized plate (local)

fendi luck

fensir (sg./pl.) pencil

fenti paint (n.)

fi in, into, at; there is . . .
 ____ *badal* instead of
 ____ *baṭin sana* in the course of a year
 ____ *bukān* instead of
 ____ *dafti* in my house
 ____ *galbi* in my opinion
 ____ *hāl addu/inya* common
 ____ *'agil* according to
 ____ *'aḷḷa* (By) God!
 ____ *'ēlti* in my youth
 ____ *kulli hāl* in any case
 (____ *l)gafa* behind, in back of
 ____ *l'āda* customarily
 ____ *lubba* inside, through
 ____ *marādi* in my opinion
 ____ (*muddit*) *'umiri* in my life
 ____ *sabab* because
 ____ *sāta bas* in a short time, immediately
 ____ *šān da* therefore
 ____ *šān šinu* because of what?
 ____ *šōfi* in my opinion
 ____ *zamān kūre* in olden times
 ____ *zanni* in my opinion

fiḍḍe silver

fihim ~ *faham* intelligence

fihim, bifham understand

fiǰǰe open space

fikir thought, idea, opinion
 ____, *bifkir* ~ *bufkur* (*l-*) care, take care of, look after

fīl, (pl.) *fayala* elephant

fi/ulān, -a so-and-so, what's-his-name

fīl(i), (pl.) *fayala* fireplace, kitchen
 ____ *innār* fireplace

fillēl at night

filwaqa/it on time

fin, ____ *ǰinnāt* because
 ____ *subbadda* therefore
 ____/*lin sub(b)āṭ* because, in order to

finǰāl, (pl.) *fanāǰīl* cup
 ____ *hana kōfi* cup of coffee

finšān because, in order to

f(i)rāš, -āt saddle blanket
 ____ *almōt* spreading mats for funeral ceremony

firi(h), bifra(h) become happy

firkīye, -āt farm (used only in dry season)

fitine conspiracy, gossip

flawa flower

flūs money

fōg on, against, through, up, concerning, about
  ___ *alwaqa/it* on time
  ___ *assarti* (at the) same time, on time
  ___ -(*āni*) above, on top, upper, upstairs

forforá, (pl.) *forforīyāt* girl approximately 12-15 years old

forfōri, (pl.) *forfōrīn* boy approximately 13-15 years old

fōtiskum Potiskum (city in N.E. Nigeria)

fōtō photograph

fuḍula, (pl.) *fiḍal* remainder, rest

fūfu disease of cattle

fuǰūr 4:00 to 6:00 A.M.

fūl groundnut(s)

funduk, (pl.) *fanādik* bowl for pounding guinea corn

furša ~ *frāš,* -*āt* mat

furšá, -*āt* brush (n.)

fūt dāxil Come inside!

fuṭura four handfuls of guinea corn or other grain, given to the poor after Ramadan

G

gabaḍ, bugubuḍ seize

gabaká, (coll.) *gabak* local cloth

gābal, bigābil face, meet

gabaṭ, bugubuṭ catch, seize

gabba collar of native shirt

gabbal, bigabbil (*min*) come back, return; bring back

gabil dugō first of all

gabīl, -e, -īn, -āt enemy, antonym
 ____ (m), (pl.) *gabāyil* (fellow) inhabitant, co-inhabitant, partner

gabul (*ma*) before, in the past; used to (v.)
 ____ *yaǰi/biǰi* before he came

gād, bugūd lead (v.)

gadá, (pl.) *gūtān* wooden food bowl

gadāf vomit (n.)

gadar fate, fortune

gadd (d.) *-e,* (pl.) *gudūd* hole
 ____ *al'ibre/alxayāṭa* eye of a needle
 ____ *almunxur,* (d.) *gadde lmunxur* nostril

gadda, bigidd ~ *bugudd* make a hole in s.t.

gaddaf, bigaddif vomit

gaddam bigaddim go before, go in front of, see s.o. off; offer; make s.t. old by use

gaddūm(*a*), (pl.) *gadādīm* mouth (anat.)

gadé (any)more, again, another; never
 (____) *kulla* again

gadīm, -e, -īn, -āt, (comm. pl.) *gudum* old, ancient (inanim.)

gadīr ~ *gādir, -e, -īn, -āt* able, capable; can

gadra kind of monkey

gadrān, -a, -īn, -āt able

gadrūm guardroom, prison

gadū (sg./pl.) wild boar

gafa behind, in back of
 ____ *da* after this
 ____ *rragaba* nape

gāfara Danger!/Excuse me!/Pardon (me)!

gafas (sg./pl.) wooden cage

gafāy in back of me

gafgal (no pl.) digging stick

gaha, bugu cough

gahawa coffee

ga'ad, būgad ~ *bugod* remain, stay
 ____, ____ *le'albarra* go to the toilet
 ____, *bugud* sit, live
 ____, ____ + impf. begin (to)
 ____ *bibki* He began to cry.
 ____ + impf./pf. just (adv.)

ga'ar, (pl.) *gu'urre* origin, tribe
 ____ *anna'āla* shoe sole
 ____ *aššadara* tree trunk

ga'ar, biǰar roar

ga'átt bākul I have just eaten.

ga''ad, biga''id seat s.o., appoint
 ____ *fōg wirka* put s.o. on one's lap

ga''ādá, -āt round stool (for women's use only)

gā'id, ____ + impf. continue (to); now, presently
 ____, *gāyde, gāydīn, gāydāt sākit* unemployed

gaǰagīr kind of animal

gaǰam, buguǰum cut, bite into

gāǰi Gaji (p.n.m., nickname)
 ____ *-ye* Gajiye (p.n.f., nickname)

gāk magpie

gāl, bi/ugūl say

gala, bigla get s.o. back
 ___, *bigli* cook, fry (meat or guinea corn)

gāla, bugūla ʾāxir repeat

galab, biglib allow (tell) s.o. to return
 ___, *bugulub* bring or take back, return
 ___, *alxēl* race course

galam, bugulum fell (a tree)

galba, ___ *angaṭa* be afraid
 ___ *ʾabyad* I like him.
 ___ *ʾazrag* I hate him.
 ___ *laffat,* ___ *tiliff* have a hot temper
 ___ *waǰā,* ___ *biwāǰ(h)i* become angry

galib, (pls.) *-āt* ~ *gulūb* heart
 ___ + pron. suff. + *abyaḍ* very happy

galīl, -e, -īn, -āt few

galīsa cassava

galla bēḍa white guinea corn

gallab, bigallib race; rest

gallābi, (pl.) *gallābīn* leather repairman, cobbler

gallam, bigallim allaham cut meat

gallāyá, -āt (metal) pan

gam wheat

gamar (no pl.) moon

gamaṭ, bigmiṭ swaddle

gambaru Gambaru (Arabic-speaking town in N.E. Nigeria)

gambāy, -e, -īn, -āt old (anim.)

gamē kind of tree, stick

gamīs, (pl.) *gumsān* gown

gamma (no impf.) break out; begin (to)
 ___, *bigūm* grow (intr.)
 ___, *bugūm* get up, stand (erect); (+ v.) start to do s.t.
 ___ *bibki* He started to cry.

gammak, bigammik doze (off)

gammēt babki I started to cry.

gammō bihaǰǰu They started talking.

gammō biyākulu They started eating.

gamūlá ~ *gamulāyá,* (coll.) *gamūl* body louse

gāmūs, (pl.) *gawāmīs* dictionary

ganā bamboo

ganas, bugnus hunt

ganaṭ̈, bugunuṭ̈ ~ *biginiṭ̈* groan out of pain (e.g., in childbirth)

gandas, bigandis slice

gandūl, (pl.) *ganādīl* ear of corn, portion of guinea corn

gangá, (pl.) *ganāgi* kind of small drum, tambourine

ganʾān, -a, -īn, -āt satisfied

ganīs hunt(ing)

gānis ~ *gannās, -īn* hunter

ganīṭ̈ groan (n.)

ganṭūr, (pl.) *ganāṭīr* anthill

ganyé, (coll.) *ganye* leaf

gara, bigra make s.o. abstain
 ___, *bigri* study, read
 ___, *bigra nafsa* feed oneself

gará, (pl.) *girē* calabash
 ___ *wāhade hīl gōro* one calabash (100) of kola nuts

gāra, bigāri stop s.o. from doing s.t.

gārab, bigārib come near

garas, bugrus pinch

gārat arrās (no pl.) skull

garbal, bigarbil sift

garēt bidāt almaktūb da I read the beginning of this book.

garfá, -āt calabash for selling guinea corn

gargar, (coll.) *garāgir* type of dark brown fish

gargūr, (pl.) *garāgīr* snail

gāri, gāre, (pl.) *gurre* great, huge, fat; Nigerian-type foods (particularly Yoruba and Ibo)

garīb, -e, -īn, -āt (*min*) near, soon

garmān, -a, -īn, -āt (*l-*) longing or yearning (for/to)

garn, (pl.) *gurūn* (animal) horn, flute

garnūk (sg./pl.) crane (ornith.)

garra, bigarri teach (from books mainly)

garrab + impf. nearly
  addūt garrab bumūt The lion nearly died.

garraf, bigarrif peel (v.)

garras, bigarris pinch

garu wall (of small round hut)

garwa strong wind during harvest time

garwa, (d.) *-tēn* (no pl.) large tin container (for carrying water on a cowlstaff)

garwá four-gallon tin (usually for oil)

garwāy, (pl.) *garwa* merchant with oxen or donkeys, who sells groundnuts, guinea corn or millet

gasa'ān kind of dance

gasam, bugusum divide, share

gāsam, bigāsim divide, come to the middle of s.t.

gāsi, -ye, -yīn, -yāt difficult, hard, complicated; expensive, high(-priced)

gassa, buguss cut open, cut one's finger, skin
  ___ *lxabar* cut one's story short

gassam, bigassim share

gassar, bigassir be small or insufficient, be unable to, fail
  ___ *ma bikaffi lmāl da* He failed to pay the money.
  ___ *ma binši* He failed to go.

gašša, bugušš sweep

gaššá, (coll.) *ga/ešš* grass, straw

gaššāšá, (pl.) *-āt* broom, rake

gaṭa, bigṭa cut (repeatedly), abuse, gossip
  ___ *allaham* cut meat
  ___ *alwa'ad* break one's promise

gaṭā rheum (from the eye)

gaṭa'a, bigṭa cross, cut across
  ___ *ragabta* slit s.o.'s throat
  ___ *rijil* take a shortcut

gaṭar, (pl.) *guṭār* train

gaṭīye libel, slander (n.)

gaṭṭa, bigaṭṭi cut across, cross, transport; cover

gaṭṭāf, -īn fingernail clippers

gaṭṭa('a), (pl.) *gaṭṭāyāt* blanket

gaṭṭāy, -a, -īn, -āt gossiper

gaw kind of grass in bush

gawi, -ye, -gawīn, -āt strong

gawwa, bigawwi galba make up one's mind

gawwād, -a, -īn, -āt leader

gawwāl, -a, -īn, -āt liar, slanderer

gawwam, bigawwim build, stack upright; wake s.o. up

gayál, (pl.) *gayaltu 'āfi* Good day!/Good afternoon!

gāyam, bigāyim wake s.o. up

gāyid, gāyde, (pl.) *guwwād* leader

gāy/'im, gāyme, -īn, -āt departing, leaving; vertical

gāyimni Wake me up!

gǟyle noon, 10:00 A.M. to 12:00 P.M.

gayyal, bigayyil spend the day

gayyam, bigayyim wake s.o. up

gazzāzá, -āt bottle, glass
  ___ *-t 'alme* water bottle
  ___ *umurta* glass

ge discharge from a boil, pus

gēd, (pl.) *guyūd* rope for tying a donkey's front legs

giddām (in) front (of), next to, (on the other) side (of), future
  ___ *-i* first, primary
  ___ *-īyāt* front teeth

gidi (no pl.) antelope

gidim, bigdam be(come) or grow old, age (inanim.)

gidir, bu/igdar be able to
  ___ *buktub* He was able to write.
  ___ *garēt* You were able to read.

gilē (sg./pl.) newly-cleared farm

gille shortage (of), lack (of), the act of having little, poverty

gillēyil, gillēle, -īn, -āt short person

gim(i)rīye, (colls.) *gi/umre/i* dove, wild pigeon
___ *hamām* pigeon (gen.)

girāfi, girāfīye, girāfīn, -īyāt generous, kind

girāya, (pl.) *girāt* studies, study(ing)

girbe, (pl.) *girāb* leather bag for carrying food or water

girbēge, (pls.) *-āt* ~ *ǰarābīg* handbag

girfé, (coll.) *girf* bark (bot.), eggshell

girib, bigrab go near

girim, bigaram (*l-*) long or yearn for

gisayyir, gisayyre, (pls.) *-īn* ~ *gusār, -āt* short, small, shallow; ninth month (of Islamic lunar calendar)

gisim, (pl.) *gismāt* share

giṭṭé, (coll.) *giṭṭ* wildcat

giyām departure

glās electric light bulb or socket, electricity

gōga, bigōgi carry on one's back

gōke (no pl.) tortoise

gōl (no pl.) decision; rumor

gōlalá tin

gongé Gonge (p.n.m.)

gongo (*l'ēš*) leftover gruel dried in pot

gōni, (pl.) *gawana* expert, Koranic scholar

gōrá, (coll.) *gōro* kola nut

gōrē, (pl.) *gōreyāt* island

gorongó (sg./pl.) betel nut

gōṭar, bugōṭir (*min*) go (away), leave

gōz, (pl.) *gīzān* bow; sandy place; ghost town

gūba leprosy

gudra ability, power, strength
___ *ke ma 'inda* He didn't have any strength left.

guha cough (n.)

guǰǰa hair (on man's head)

gūl assahī digé Tell only the truth!

gūl ley assahī Tell me the truth!

gūlu lēna Tell/Show us!

gulumá, (coll.) *gulum* kind of tree in bush

gum abuk, gummi abki, gummu abku, gumman abkan Start crying!

gumār gambling

gumāš yard (measure)

gumbul, (pl.) *ganābul* water gourd

gumguma, -āt skull

gurāsa flat bread

gurbāl, (pl.) *garābīl* big woven serving plate, sieve

gurbi, (pl.) *garaba* relative

gurdo (no pls.) profit, marked-up price

gurfo Gurfo (village in N.E. Nigeria)

gurs cost, price

gurus, (pl.) *grūs* silver money used for necklaces or rings; money

gusūr upstairs (second floor)

guṭrān smell of fire with oil

guṭṭīyé, (pl.) *gaṭṭāṭi* tuft of grass on grass hut roof; tuft of hair

guṭuná, (coll.) *guṭun* cotton

H

ha negative particle

ha ~ *hā(y)* Oh!

haba, behebi crawl

habas, bihebas imprison

habba, (pl.) *hubūb* pill, tablet

habba, buhubb like, love; arouse, awaken

habbāb, -a, -īn, -āt owner; belonging to, owned by
 ____ *bētak* wife (idiomatic)
 ____ *-ta fāṭime* It belongs to Fatime.

habbās, -īn jailor

habil, (pl.) *hubāl* rope

habīl, -e, -īn, -āt stupid

habyān, -a, -īn, -āt crawling

hadar, bēhidir (fōg) shout at s.o.

hadd, (pl.) *hudūd* border, boundary

hadda, bihidd ~ *buhudd (l-)* mourn

hadda(la) before, ago
 —— *šifta ʾindina xamsa yōm* I saw him five days ago.
 ____ *wildōha ʾayyōm ʾindaha ʾašara sana* She was born ten years ago today.

hadda madda very fast (e.g., as a galloping horse)

haddād(i), haddāde, -īn, -āt blacksmith
 ____ *hana ddahab* goldsmith
 ____ *hana lfiḍḍe* silversmith

haddas, bihaddis tell, converse, communicate, sit down and talk

hādi only; then, and then; all right

hadīd iron (metal)
 ____ *-e* one piece of iron

hadīr thunder

hadīs conversation; tradition of the Prophet

haḍan, bihaḍan embrace, carry under the arm

haḍḍar, bihaḍḍir prepare

hāḍir, -e, -īn, -āt present (adj.)

hāf, buhūf spoil (intr.)

hafad, bihefad care, take care of, keep, save

hafar, bihefar dig

hāfar, bihāfir dig

hafaz, bihēfiz learn the Koran by heart

haffār, -īn digger

hafiyān, hafyāna, -īn, -āt rough (of skin)

hāg, buhūg encircle, surround, complete a cycle

hagar, bihēgir ~ *beheger* ~ *bihegar* scorn, despise, disobey

hagg belonging to

haggá, (coll.) *hagg,* (pl.) *hugūg* portion, share

(hā)hāk, -i, -u, -an hu da Take this!/Here it is!

hāʾil, -e, -īn, -āt dangerous, awesome

hāǰa, -āt thing; something

haǰab, bēǰib guard s.t. by asking a Muslim religious teacher (leader) to pray for its safety

haǰam, bēǰam attack

haǰar, (pls.) *hi/uǰār* ~ *huǰūr* mountain, stone, rock
haǰar hana toč flashlight bulb

hāǰaz, bihāǰiz interfere

hāǰira another

ha/iǰirāni, ha/iǰirānīye, ha/iǰirānīn, -āt next

haǰǰa, bihaǰǰi tell a story

haǰǰāǰá, -āt fan, ventilator

hajjar, bihajjir restrain; beg

hajūj strong wind

hāk ley Tell me!

hāka, bihāki lxabar tell a story

hakam, behekam rule, punish

hākam, bihākim fine

hakēf How come?/Why?

hakīm, -īn judge (n.)

hākim, -e, hukkām, -āt chief, ruler, governor

hakk, (pl.) *hukūk* scratch

hakka, buhukk scratch, sharpen, erase

hāl, (pl.) *hawāyl* mood

hāl(a), (pl.) *ahawāl* case, state, condition, reputation
hāla kwayse His reputation is good.

halab, bēlib milk (v.)

halaf, bēlif (ba'aḷḷa) swear (by God)
___ *(baz)zur* perjure

halagá, -āt saddle (of grass)

halāl lawful

(h)alāwa, -āt candy, sweets

halīb boiled milk

halla, bihill untie; come out (of the moon)

hallab, bihellib (fi) milk (v.)

hallaf, bihallif make s.o. swear

hallak, bihallik be dangerous; endanger

hallāka Danger!

hallūf, (pl.) *halālīf* wild pig or boar

hama, (pl.) *humyān* brother-in-law, husband's friend
___ *-'i* my brother-in-law

hāma, bihāmi (l-) help

hamad, bihēmid thank

hamaji, hamajīye, hamaj, hamajīyāt half-breed (person with Arab mother and non-Arab father, usually a Kanuri)

hamāk your brother-in-law

hamal, bihamal carry
___, (pl.) *humulān* baby lamb

hamāmá, (coll.) *hamām* pet pigeon

hamār twilight

hamarāyá, (coll.) *hamra* baobab tree

hamātak your sister-in-law

hamati my sister-in-law

hamati wēn alharrā di How about this heat?

hamāyá, -āt sister-in-law, wife's friend

hambak handbag

hāmi, -ye, -yīn, -yāt fertile, rich (of soil); hot; hard worker

hāmiḍ, hāmḍe, -īn, -āt acid(ic), sour

hamīm, -e, -īn, -āt diligent, energetic

hamīye (no pl.) protection

hamm, (pl.) *humūm* sorrow, worry, anxiety

hammal, bihammil load, make carry
___ *wičih* be able to face s.o.

hammāl, -a, -īn, -āt carrier, porter

hammam, bihammim annoy, tease

hammar, bihammir become or dye red
___ *(l-)* look or stare at s.o.

hamu heat (n.)

hana, hīl, hinē, hille (made) of, belonging to, (for) the purpose of
___ *ddihik* funny
___ *'ašara haw wāhid* eleventh
___ *l'āda* ordinary
(___) *minē* who(se) (interr.)
___ *sirr/aširr* confidential

hanāha, (pl.) *hinayyaha* hers, its (f.)

hanāhin, (pl.) *hinnayyihin* theirs (f.)

hanāhu, (pl.) *hinayya* his, its (m.)

hanāhum, (pl.) *hinnayyuhum* theirs (m.)

hanak, (pl.) *hunukke* jaw, palate

hanāk, (pl.) *hinēyak* yours (m. sg.)

hanākan, (pl.) *hinayykan* yours (f.pl.)

hanāki, (pl.) *hinayyki* yours (f.sg.)

hanāku, (pl.) *hinayyku* yours (m.pl.)

hanāna, (pl.) *hinayyna* our(s)

hanāy, (pl.) *hineyyi* mine (pron.)

hanhan, bihanhin neigh

hanhān neigh(ing)

hankaršīf handkerchief (term used by men)

hanna, buhunn feel sorry for

hannas, bihannis persuade s.o. (to do s.t. good)

hanūn, -a, -īn, -āt merciful

haqqaq, bihaqqiq prove

har abadá never

hārá, (pl.) *hawāri* back yard

hārab, bihārib fight with

haraka, -āt movement; business (matter)

haram, (pl.) *ahrām* (Egyptian) pyramid

harām forbidden

harāmi, -ye, -harāmīn, -āt wicked

haran, biheran not budge from a price (when bargaining)
 ___ *fōg ʾarbaʾa naira* He wouldn't budge from ₦4.

harāra pain

hararāt (no sg.) spices

haras, biheras ~ *bēras* look at s.o., watch, guard; frown
 ___ *beʾēna alfasile* look at s.o. with distaste

harat, biherit (3rd m.pl. *biyertu*) dig, hoe, cultivate

harba, (pl.) *hirāb* spear, war

harf, (pl.) *hurūf* letter (of alphabet)

harīb, -e, -īn, -āt enemy

harīge (no pl.) fire in the bush (for agricultural purposes)

harīr silk

harīs, -e, -īn, -āt miser(ly), stingy

hāris ~ *harrās,* (pl.) *-īn* guard, watchman

harǰa, -āt fight, quarrel (n.)

harǰān, -a, -īn, -āt very angry

hārr, -a, -īn, -āt hot, spicy, hot-headed

harrā (no pl.) sun

harrag, biherrig roast; fire pottery

harrak, biharrik move; put food on a cooking grate

harram, biharrim respect (v.)

harrān balky horse

harrar, biharrir heat; free, liberate

harrās, -īn watchman, guard

harraš, biharriš provoke

harrāt(i), -a, -īn, -āt farmer

harrā(yá) heat (n.)

harsam, biharsim prevent s.o. from an important matter

harsūm obstacle

hasab, bēsib compute, figure

hasad, bihesad ~ *bēsid* be jealous, envious or stingy

hasal, bēsal happen

hasan(a) Hassan (p.n.m.)

hasībe small snake (found in houses)

hāsid, -e, -īn, -āt jealous, envious, stingy

haskanité, (coll.) *haskanit* kind of grass with sharp thorns

hāss, (pl.) *hawāss* sense

hassa, bihiss feel, realize

hassa (da) immediately, (right) now
 ___ *san(a)tēn* two years ago

hassa hassa suddenly

hassal, bihassil get, obtain, produce

hassūd, -a, -īn, -āt spiteful

hasūd, -e, -īn, -āt envy, envious, jealous(y), stinginess, stingy

hašīš grass

haššā Sorry!

hatta ~ *hassa* now; until, so that
___ *ʾabadá* never

hatta, bihitt brush; knock down (as fruit from a tree)

hattaš, bihattiš sneeze

h/xaṭab wood

h/xaṭṭa, buh/xuṭṭ build, put (up)
___ *aššarr* (*fōg*) blame

ha(*w*) and (then), while, when

hawā atmosphere

hāwag, bihāwig surround

hawān, -a, -īn, -āt bad, no(t) good, naughty, useless

hawāri fence

hawsa Hausa (language/people)

hawwag, bihawwig surround, fence around

hawwāt, -īn fisherman

hawwaṭ, bihawwiṭ fish (v.)

haxx, (pl.) *huqūq* right (n.)

hāy Hey!/Oh!/You!
___ *assafi* Hey, stupid!
___ *haylati* Oh, I'm enjoying it!

hāyif, hāyfe, -īn, -āt useless person

hāyig, hāyge, -īn, -āt round, encircling, around

hāyiš, -e, -īn, -āt conceited

hāyō It's all over/finished.

hayy, -e, -īn, -āt alive, living

hayya, bihayyi scare away

hayyāt katīrāt frequently, often

hayyāt tinēn ~ *hayyatēn* twice

hayye, -āt instance, time, occasion
___ *wāhade* once
___ *wāhade maʾa lmarfāʾīn kulla sawwaha* Do it one time with a hyena! [said to s.o. not trustworthy]

hayyin, hayne, -īn, -āt a little, small quantity; easy, simple

hazalá, (pl.) *huzūl* bump (in a road), valley

hazza, buhuzz ~ *bihizz* shake (tr.)

hēl power, strength; must, be compulsory
___ *banši* I must go.
___ *fōg* be necessary
___ *fōgi nimši* It is necessary for me to go.
___ *nādum biyāṭi zakāt* It is compulsory for a person to give alms.

helū, helwe, -īn, -āt comfort, pleasure, happiness; pleasant, pleasing, nice, delicious, sweet
___ *l-* enjoy
___ *ley* I enjoy it.

helweye (f.sg.) very sweet

hēṭ, (pl.) *huyūṭ* wall (of house)

hi she
___ *di seme/semha* She is good.

hibin, (pl.) *hubūn* boil

hiḍir, bēḍir be present

higre scorn, lack of respect, disobedience

hiǰe (no pl.) riddle

hiǰēr, -āt pebble, stone

hiǰil, (pl.) *huǰūl* anklet

hiǰiliǰé, (coll.) *hiǰiliǰ* desert date palm or fruit thereof

hiǰǰ hadj (pilgrimage to Mecca)

hiǰǰé, (pl.) *hiǰe* story, tale

hikāyá, -āt story, tale

hīké, -āt story, tale

hikima wisdom

hīl, (pl.) *halāl* belonging to

hilāl aššahar new moon/month

hilbe šēbe seeds mixed with oil

hīle, (pl.) *hawāyil* suggestion

hilēle, -āt small village

hilim (no pl.) dream
___, *bēlam* dream (v.)

hille, (pl.) *hallāl* village, town, city

hīl(*le*) *ʾašara haw wāhid* eleventh

hillinna bas alkabīre fi nayǰirya Our town is the biggest in Nigeria.

himēyir, (f.) *himēre* small donkey

himil, bēhamal (*b*-) endure, suffer (with)

himilat, tīmil be(come) pregnant

himma diligence, energy

himrá, (coll.) *hamra* antelope

hināk (over) there

hinē ʾašara haw wāhid eleventh

hinēn here
  ___ *bas* right here

hinne leaves soaked in water then used as bracelets and anklets by women

hinne/a they (f.pl.)

hinnīye (no pl.) pity, sympathy

hirāta agriculture, cultivation

hirig, behereg burn oneself

hisāb arithmetic

hīsān, (pl.) *xēl* horse, stallion

hisib, bēsib (but 2nd m.sg./3rd f.sg.) *tāsib* think, assume, reckon

hiss, (pl.) *husūs* ~ *hasasa* voice

hissa ankasar, ___ *binkasir* be hoarse

hōbi kind of song (sung by men only)

hōl, (pl.) *hīlān* year

hōš, (pl.) *hīšān* hut, house

hōtēl, -āt hotel

hōṭ, (pl.) *hīṭān* water tank, cistern, small dam

hu he
  ___ *baʾagla* He is intelligent.
  ___ *bas arrāǰil da* This man is the only one.
  ___ *da ʾaǰab* It's a miracle./This is a surprise.
  (___) *da ʾēb lēk/fōgak* Shame on you!
  ___ *da kēf* How is this possible?
  ___ *gāʾid bibki* He continued to cry./He is crying (now).
  ___ *gāʾid bunūm* He is (still) asleep.
  ___ *gāʾid helū lēya* He is living in comfort.
  ___ *hādi bikšāha* Only he can find it.
  ___ *hargān* He burned himself.
  ___ *ʾangara lalmamša* He avoided going.
  ___ *ʾinda ǰanīye kabīre* He is a criminal.
  ___ *ʾinda karambāni bilēn* He is very curious.
  ___ *lamma māla finšān bidawwir bišri lēya mobilet* He saved his money in order to buy a motorcycle.
  ___ *lammāna anīna čat* He gathered us all together.
  ___ *marḍān miṭawwil* ~ ___ *marḍān yōmāt katīrāt* He was sick for a long time.
  ___ *nādum bihēla* He is a strong man.
  ___ *ṭān alwal da ʾibri* He vaccinated the boy.
  ___ *ye* he himself

hubāl anniʾille shoelaces

hubb liking, love

hubbini Wake me up!

huḍūr presence

hufra, (pl.) *hufār* hole

huǰǰá ~ *hūǰá, -āt* cause, reason, excuse

hukum judgment

hūl belonging to

humār, (pls.) *humurre* ~ *hamīr* donkey

humma they (m.pl.)
  ___ *dōla gabala* They are similar.
  ___ *gālō salām labaʾaḍhum* They say hello to each other.
  ___ *kān farhānīn* They were happy.
  ___ *ye* they themselves

hurār feces
  ___ *aǰǰidād* chicken droppings

hurma respect (n.)

hurr, -a, -īn, -āt free (adj.)

hurrīye freedom

husūl (no pl.) event, happening

hūt yābis dried fish

I

-i ~ -y my

ibāda worship (n.)
 ___ *(-t) alla* worship of God

iblīs, (pl.) *abālīs* devil, Satan

ibre/i, (pl.) *ibar* injection, needle

īd, (pl.) *ayada* festival
 ___ *addihīye* (same as *īd alkabīr*)
 (___ *al)faṭir* Eid Alfatir (Muslim holiday); eleventh month (of Islamic lunar calendar)
 ___ *alkabīr* Eid Alkabir (Muslim holiday/ festival in which one kills goats and rams, two months after Ramadan); first month (of Islamic lunar calendar)
 ___ *almawlūd* Eid Almawlud (Muslim holiday); fourth month (of Islamic lunar calendar)

īd (f.), (ds.) *ēdē(n),* (pl.) *ēde* hand, arm; handwriting; short-sleeved
 ___ *albarrād* teapot handle
 ___ *alfīl,* (pl.) *eyad alfayala* elephant trunk

ijile, (pls.) *ajāl(āt),* (coll.) *ijil* calf (bovine)

ijiz, bējaz grow old (of women)

ijizat, tējaz be(come) old, age (anim. – of women)

ijwād, (pl.) *ajāwīd* elder

ikko Lagos

ila to

ilim knowledge

ilīye, (pl.) *alāli* small grass hut, stall, small shop
 ___ *-t assūg* market hut or stall

illa/e only (one), except
 ___ *ʾana bas* only me

illalʾāfi The family is fine.

ille until

ima, bēma become blind

imām imam

īmān faith

i/amm, (pls.) *umumme ~ amām* paternal uncle

imme people, tribe

immiti my people/tribe

imta when (conj.)

imtihān, -āt examination, test

in zēn You will see the consequences!

ind- have, possess
 ___ + *daraja* respectable
 ___ *(l-)* have, possess
 ___ + *qarad* intend
 ___ + *šaʾāwa* interesting
 ___ + *tamtāmá* stammer, stutter
 ___ + *ṭāná* wounded

inda, ___ *daraja* crucial, important
 ___ *gurdo* He always marks up the price.
 ___ *ʾagil* He is intelligent.
 ___ *rīš/sāʾa* He is lucky.

indak filūs wa Do you have money?

indi, ___ *kalām bajlus ʾalēka* I have s.t. to tell you.
 ___ *māl ašiya min hanāk* I have more money than you.
 ___ *rafīg bunādu ma/uhamme/ad* I have a friend called Muhammad.
 ___ *rāy wāhid ke nisawwī* I have an idea to put into action.
 ___ *ṭūla ma šiftak* I haven't seen you in a long time.

īne continuous heavy rain, very heavy rainy season (July-August)

insāni, (pl.) *insān* human being

inšān because

inta (m.sg.), *intum* (m.pl.), *inti* (f.sg.), *intan* (f.pl.) you
 ___ *hawāylak katīrāt* You are very busy./ You have many moods.
 ___ *hēl tigír* You must study!
 ___ *ʾāfi wal̤la* Are you well?
 ___ *min wēn* Where are you from?

intaha, -āt test, examination

intāri Behold!/Indeed! (interjection denoting surprise)
 ___ *ddūt* Behold! It is the lion!

inti you (f.sg.)
 ___ *bitt maknūsa tara* You're a bad girl, aren't you?
 ___ *tigír/ ʾagir zēn kan tidawwir tākul alʾintaha* You ought to study more if you want to pass the examination.

irfe knowledge

irg kind of leg disease

irg, (pl.) *urūg* tree root

irid, bērid run away, escape

irif, bēraf recognize s.o.
 ___, *bi ʾeraf* ~ *bērif* know

irse, -āt marriage ceremony

isēy my sticks

isi, bēsi rebel (v.)

isim ~ *usum* ~ *summ,* (pl.) *asmā* name

išim, bēšam hope (v.)

ismak minē What's your name (m.sg.)?

isra ~ *isrāy* left (direction)

is(s)al ~ *as(s)al* honey

istahabal, -āt proverb

istahamma, bistahamma take a bath

istākal, bistākal be able to eat

istarāh, bista/eri(h) be at rest, relax

īšá evening (8:00 P.M. to 12:00 A.M.)

išāra, -āt signal (n.)

išé dinnertime (7:00 P.M. to 9:00 P.M.)

īše livelihood, living

išim, bēšam hope (v.)

iširīn twenty
 ___ *wāhid* twenty-one

išš Shoo!

i/aššahi tea

ištara, bišteri buy

it(i)nēn ~ *tinēn(i)* two

itir (no pl.) (good) scent, perfume

iṭiš, biṭaša be thirsty

i/uwārá, (pl.) *awāwīr* sore, wound

iya shout(ing)

(ī)yāl family, children [pl. of *wal(ad)* 'boy']
 ___ *addōm* fruit for making gruel
 ___ *aššadar almurakkibinhum (basukkur)* jam
 ___ *kada/katīrīn* many children
 ___ *-na ḍambuhum fōgna* We are responsible for our children.

īyām talāta three days

(ī)yān nās person of well-to-do family (m.pl.)

iyī, bēya be tired

izin (no pl.) *permission*

J̌

ǰā, biǰi come
  ___ *lakūzi haw/sā'it ana qaflān* He came to my house while I was asleep.

ǰāb, biǰīb (3rd m.pl. *buǰūbu*) bring
  ___ *walad* bring forth, give birth

ǰabad, bi/uǰubud pull or take out
  ___ *sēfa* draw one's sword

ǰabar, buǰubur force

ǰabba, (pl.) *ǰubūb* long shirt

ǰabbādat, (pl.) *-āt 'alme* bucket of water

ǰabbar, biǰabbir repair

ǰabīr ~ ǰābir, -e, -īn, -āt clever, wise, hard-working

ǰada'á, -āt female, girl

ǰadām, -a, -īn, -āt clever

ǰadda, biǰidd roar, shout

ǰadda, buǰudd chatter

ǰadīd, -e, (pl.) *ǰudād* new

ǰafa, (pl.) *-hāt* forehead

ǰafal, buǰuful retreat, shy away

ǰafawa ~ ǰufū, (pl.) *ǰēb* pocket

ǰāff, -e, -īn, -āt already dry

ǰaffa, biǰaffi dry (tr.)
  ___, *biǰiff* drive animals fast

ǰagandīye, -āt mandolin

ǰagǰag, biǰagǰig trot

ǰāɣ, -e, -īn, -āt poking with one's finger, tickling

ǰaɣǰaɣ kind of tree or fruit thereof

ǰaɣǰaɣ, biǰaɣǰiɣ poke with one's finger, tickle

ǰahad, biǰhad deny

ǰahāla ignorance

ǰahannam Hell

ǰāha/et, biǰāhit fight

ǰahhaz, biǰahhiz provide, supply

ǰahīl ~ ǰāhil, -e, -īn, -āt, (comm. pl.) *ǰuhhāl* ignorant

ǰāhiz, -e, -īn, -āt ready

ǰa'abá, (pls.) *-āt ~ ǰābāt* buttock(s)

ǰa'al, biǰ'al make
  ___, *biǰal* incite

ǰa'ar, biǰ'ar cry for help

ǰāǰá, (coll.) *ǰāǰa* kind of tree

ǰakka, biǰakki fill (tr.)

ǰakw(āy)á, (pl.) *ǰakāwi* hat, cap

ǰalabá, (coll.) *ǰalab,* (pl.) *ǰulubbe* (cement or mud) block, brick

ǰalad, buǰulud beat, whip, spank

ǰalāla prayer

ǰalas, biǰilis ~ buǰulus sit, sit down and talk, have a conversation, tell, speak a foreign language

ǰaldān whipping

ǰalla, biǰill polish

ǰallābi, ǰallābīye, ǰallābīyīn, -yāt Sudanese; trader

ǰallābīye, -āt big gown

ǰallal, biǰallil pray

ǰallāy, -āt (local large) toothpick

ǰama, biǰma gather, collect, store away

ǰamad, buǰ(u)mud solidify, harden, curdle, clot (blood)

ǰamā'a ~ ǰam'īye, -āt gathering, meeting, society, population, people *ǰamal,* (pls.) *ǰumāl* ~ *ǰumulle* camel

ǰāmūs, (pl.) *ǰawāmīs* water buffalo

ǰam(ba) next to, (on the other) side (of)

ǰambēn close (to)

ǰamfā(yá), -āt kind of sleeveless shirt

ǰamī together

ǰāmid, -e, -īn, -āt solid; thick (of liquids)

ǰāmiʾe, -āt mosque

ǰamǰam close (to)

ǰammad, biǰammid harden, solidify (tr.)

ǰammal, biǰammil total (v.)

ǰammām, -āt shallow well (dry in summer)

ǰamsindi kind of grass used for burning

ǰamūr charcoal fire

ǰanāba sexual intercourse

ǰanāʾiza, (pls.) *-āt* ~ *ǰanāʾiz* funeral

ǰanāza dead body, corpse

ǰandi (no pl.) soldier

ǰangá, (pl.) *xēl* mare

ǰangat albīr rope for climbing down a well

ǰangūlá, (coll.) *ǰangūl,* (pl.) *ǰanāgīl* old clothes, rags

ǰanīne, -āt woman in the early stages of pregnancy

ǰanīye, -āt guilt, crime

ǰanna (no pl.) paradise

ǰār, buǰūr (fōg) oppress

ǰār, (pls.) *ǰīrān* ~ *ǰawāri* neighbor

ǰara, biǰri run, gallop

ǰarab scabies

ǰaras (sg./pl.) bell

ǰarīde, (pl.) *ǰarāʾid* arm bone, radius; (village style) bed cover made of wood

ǰarr, (pl.) *ǰurār* small olla

ǰarr, (pl.) *ǰurūr* stripe

ǰarra, -āt earthenware jar

ǰarra, buǰurr chew (animals only)

ǰarrab, biǰarrib test (v.)

ǰarrābá, -āt test, examination

ǰarrāy, -īn (fast) runner; faster

ǰarsis, biǰarsis march

ǰarū (no pl.) cub

ǰ/šattat, bišattit spread

ǰawād, -e, -īn, -āt kind, generous

ǰawāniye, -āt kind of cloth for men

ǰawāz, -āt assafar passport

ǰāwaz, biǰāwuz provide, supply

ǰawwaz, biǰawwiz get married

ǰāy, -e, -īn, -āt coming (act. part.), future

ǰāyis My condolences!

ǰazā end, result (n.)

ǰazam, buǰuzum be reliable

ǰāzar, biǰāzar refuse (v.)

ǰāzim, ǰāzme, -īn, -āt reliable; troublemaker

ǰazma, -āt European-style shoe

ǰazza, buǰuzz cut
 ____ *algašš* cut grass
 ____ *(alqanamá)* shear (a sheep)

ǰazzāri, (pl.) *ǰazzārīn* butcher

ǰēǰi (countryside) bush; barren area

ǰenēne ~ *ǰinēna, -āt* garden

ǰēt ~ *ǰayīt* coming (n.)

ǰīb, -i, ǰūbu, ǰīban Bring!/Give!
 ____ *ley ʾalme šikk* Give me more water!
 ____ *-ha* answer to an introduction of a riddle or story (lit., 'Bring it!')

ǰidādá, (coll.) *ǰidād* hen, chicken

ǰidatti my chicken

ǰidd, (pl.) *ǰudūd* grandfather, grandparent
 ____ *ǰidd* great-grandfather, great-grandparent
 ____ *-e, -āt* grandmother

ǰ/gidi (no pl.) antelope

ǰidri smallpox

ǰigā (sg./pl.) vulture

ǰihād holy war

ǰīhe, (pl.) *ǰihāt* direction

ǰī'ān, -a, -īn, -āt hungry, starving

ǰik(k)ā(yá), (pls.) *ǰi/akāki* bag, suitcase

ǰilda hāmi He has a fever. (Lit., His skin is hot.)

ǰilde, (coll.) *ǰilid,* (pl.) *ǰulūd* (human) skin

ǰillābīye, -āt robe

ǰimmēzé, (coll.) *ǰimmēz* fig tree

ǰinā, (pl.) *ǰanāhe* (bird's) wing

ǰinn, (pl.) *ǰunūn* genie

ǰins tribe

ǰinzīr, (pl.) *ǰanāzīr* large chain

ǰirāb, (pl.) *ǰurubbe* parfleche

ǰ/girbēge, (pls.) *-āt* ~ *ǰarābīg* bag

ǰīre neighborhood

ǰirf, (pl.) *ǰurūf* mud dam wall

ǰir/lgi railway, train

ǰisim (no pl.) body

ǰīt min dār wēn(i) ~ *ǰīt min yēn* Where are you from?

ǰītan ǰīt(an) Greetings! (woman to woman)

ǰīze, -āt marriage

ǰizze dead body, corpse

ǰo'ar cry(ing)

ǰōkar, biǰōkar hop

ǰōki (no pl.) chameleon

ǰoqāná, (coll.) *ǰoqān* ebony

ǰōr injustice, oppression

ǰōz husband
____ *-á, -āt* wife, woman

ǰu drought, famine, hunger

ǰubā('a) (no pl.) tax

ǰufū ~ *ǰafawa,* (pl.) *ǰēb* pocket

ǰufū'i ~ *ǰīfīti* my pocket

ǰugūdiyé (no pl.) dagger

ǰumla, -āt total (n.)
____ *-t annās* all the people

ǰungulo (no pl.) rainbow

ǰu/awāb, (pls.) *-āt* ~ *ǰuwubbe* answer; letter

ǰuwād, (pl.) *xēl* horse

ǰuzū, (d.) *ǰuzu'ēn* (no pl.) part

K

ka bas but; for no reason at all
  ___ *bamši* I will go for no reason at all.

kabadbadi kind of tree

kabas, bukubus pounce on, attack

kabba, bukubb ladle (v.)

kabbar, bikabbir appoint

kabēto gourd (plant)

kabīr, -e, -īn, -āt, (comm. pl.) *kubār* ~ *kubbārīye* big, thick; important, old (anim.), chief, ruler, boss, overseer, president
  ___ *alfaqara* headmaster

kabiš, (pl.) *kubšān* ram

kāči cloth

kāčiyé, (coll.) *kāči* guinea fowl

kada, kōmīn, -āt many
  ___ *nnās* ~ *nàs katīrīn* many people

kadāde countryside

kadamōl, (pl.) *kadāmīl* turban

kadanki, -yāt border, boundary

kadar, (pl.) *kudurre* (little) house

kadar (*ma*) before

kadār, (pls.) *-āt* ~ *kudurre* pony

kadda, bukudd (*fi*) go around

kaddāb, -e, -īn, -āt habitual liar

kaddad, bikaddid take s.o. around

kādib false

kadkad aššukur recommendation

kadkadat addaxalān ticket (for admission)

kafa upside down
  ___, *bifka* turn upside down

kafā ~ *kaffáh* Enough!

kaff (f.), (d.) *-ēn,* (pls.) *kufū/āf* palm (of hand)

kaffa, bikaffi pay, repay
  ___, *bukuff* border (v.)

kafintay, -īn carpenter

kāfir, -e, kuffār, kāfirāt infidel, non-believer

kāfōr camphor

kaftān, -āt gown

kā'a (no pl.) egg yolk

ka'ab (f.), (pl.) *ku'ubbe* heel (of foot or shoe)

kājá, (coll.) *kāja* goat (gen.)

kajar, bukujur bend (tr.)

kajiji ngūru kind of grass for burning

kajja, bukujj čēl (*l-*) set a trap

kāk sweetened food made from wheat

kakā grandfather

kāl at all
  ___ *alme mā fi* ~ *alme* ___ *mā fi* There is no water at all.
  ___ *xumāma dugō bā'a* He measured his goods before he sold them.

kāl, bikīl measure

kala Kala (Arabic-speaking village in N.E. Nigeria)

kala kind of bird

kalabūs fez, tarboosh

kalām, -āt talk, speech, word, language, proverb, opinion, decision
  ___ *alfasāha* proverb
  ___ *al'inglīz* English language
  ___ *annaṣāra* English language
  ___ *arab* Arab(ic) language
  (___) *assiyāsa* politics
  ___ *barno* Kanuri language
  (___) *b(i)rāya ke* nonsense
  ___ (*dunya*) trouble

___ *fallāta* Fulani language
___ *fi baṭinum kalām* proverb
___ *xāli* nonsense

kālam, bikālim cause trouble; be in trouble

kalāwa Sorry!
___, *-āt* consolation

kalb, (pl.) *kilāb* dog
___ *alganīs* hunting dog
___ *alkūzi* beam (in a house)
___ *alwādi* lion

kalēl, (pl.) *kalālil* small pot

kali/ekukwa (no pl.) baobab tree

kalkal correct, exactly, equally, alright, quite so

kall very (much)

kallābá ~ *karrābá, -āt* pincers, tongs

kallam, bikallim say

ka/ilma, (pl.) *kal(i)māt* word

kaltūma Kaltuma (p.n.f.)

kam how much?, how many?; unless
___ *bisawwi* How much does it cost?
___ *hu da kam* How much is it?

kā̀m ~ *kā̀n* if

kamad, bukumud squeeze (s.t.) into (a container)

kamān also

kambal, bikambil pile up, stack, gather wood

kambūl, (pl.) *kanābīl* heap, pile

kamfūd bran

kamfūs waist cloth for women

kāmil absolutely, positively

kammal, bikammil be finished

kammūná, (coll.) *kammūn* kind of perfume

kan/m when (conj.)

kān was [rare]

kā̀n if
___ *hu ǯā kulla ma bamšī* Even if he comes, I won't go.
___ *šifta kan baǯi* If I see him, then I will come.
___ *ya dugut* up until now

kān, bukūn happen

kananzīr kerosene

kandak, bikandak assemble

kandir (no pl.) candle

kanīs kanīs something

kanǯar, bikanǯir bend, curve (tr. /intr.)

kāno Kano (capital of Hausaland)

kanti shop; canteen

kara, bikra dislike, hate

kara/ib ~ *qara/ib, buk/qrub* approach, capture, catch, (take) hold (of), overcome, acknowledge
___, *bikara/ib annār* build a fire
___, *bukrub azzukumá* catch a cold
___, *bukrub fi galba* be mean or malicious
___, *bikara/ib kurba zēn* make s.o. feel at home

karaf, bukuruf smell (for animals – tr.)

karāha hatred

karaǯ, bukuruǯ take a bite

karāma generosity

karamāy evil eye

karambāni curiosity

karas (sg./coll.) carrot

karas, bukurus take cover, hide (intr.)

karāsu kind of plant

karaz, bukuruz take cover, hide (intr.)

karba hot and stuffy

kāré material, goods; clothes; baggage
___ *lxidime* workmat

karib, bukrub watch, sit with, babysit

karīm, -e, -īn, -āt generous, kind

karko albahar riverbank

karkūr (sg./pl.) beehive

karkūr, (pl.) *karākīr* hole in a tree
___ *al'ēn* eyeball

karmé, (pl.) *kawārim* beads for large necklace

karnak (sg./pl.) big city

karnōyá, (coll.) *karno* kind of large tree

karra, bikirr tear in two (tr.)
___, *bukurr* pull out (towards)
___, *bikirr/bukurr* (*balhēl*) roar, shout

karrab, bikarrib attāba light a cigarette

karrābá ~ *kallābá, -āt* pincers, tongs

karšam, bikaršim shrink, wither (tr.)

karta (sg./pl.) (playing) card(s)

karwāl structure of two poles with a roof on which broken calabashes are placed, to keep birds away

kās, bukūs (*fī*) travel (in)

kasa, biksa/i buy clothes for s.o.

kasab, bukusub win

kasar, buk(u)sur break (tr.)
___ *al'ōda* break the law
___ *alwa'ad* break one's promise
___ (*min*) escape, run away

kaskas, bikaskis go backwards, leave without turning around; whisper

kaslān, -a, -īn, -āt lazy

kassa, bikiss move, settle (down)

kassar, bikassir break to pieces, smash, cut repeatedly

kassō dallāthum gā'idīn Then they sat down.

kaša, bikša establish, found; uncover, discover
___ (*alxumām*) unfold (clothes)

kašaf, bukšuf observe; rage

kāši open mouth

kašša, bukušš (*fōg*) scold

katab, buktub write

katal killing (n.)
___, *buktul* kill

katalō killed

kat/danká, (pl.) *kat/dank(āt)* hoe

katarko (sg./pl.) bridge

katib writing

kātib, -e, (pls.) *-īn* ~ *kuttāb, -āt* literate, writer, scribe, bookkeeper
___ *alhisāb* accountant

katīr, -e, -īn, -āt many, abundant, frequently, often
___ *-īn nās* majority (of people)

katkadá, -āt letter

katkad(āy)á, (coll.) *katkad* paper

katsina Katsina (city in N.C. Nigeria)

kattal, bikattil kill

kattar, bikattir increase (tr.)

kawa, bikwi brand, press or iron (clothes)

kawwas, bikawwis chew

kawwāy, -īn brander

kazōre Kazore (village near Kano)

ke around; out, (over) there; that (conj.)
___ *yā lhōl* for a year

kēf how?
___ *albardā di* How is the cold season?
___ *magīlku* How do you spend the day?
___/*šinu* (*min*) *ǰildak/hālak* How are you?

kēfak (*min ǰildak/hālak*) How are you?

kēfkēf ~ *kekēf* why?, how?

kēké (sg./pl.) bicycle

kēl, (pls.) *mkayala* ~ *bakāyil* kind of measure

kēsa white fine sand

kibbēšé, (coll.) *kibbēš* kind of bush

kibde, -āt ~ *kibad* liver

kibēš, -īn small ram

kibir, bukubur grow up, be(come) old, age (anim.)

kibrīye important position

kida thus

kidayyir, kidayyre, -īn, -āt small pony

kidib, bukudub lie, tell lies

kille/a also

kīlo kilogram

kilwe, (pl.) *kilāw* kidney

kimil, bukumul be finished

kindé, (pl.) *kanādi* small basket

kindikindi kind of animal

kirdi ~ *kirdāy, kirdāye, -īn, -āt* pagan

kirš (f.), (pl.) *kurūš* belly, stomach

kiskir (sg./pl.) basket

kisre/a, (pl.) *kusār* unleavened bread, kind of local bread

kiswe, (pls.) *kasāwi* ~ *kasāy* garment

kitāb, (pl.) *kutub* book

kitfe/a, (d.) *katāfe tinēn,* (colls.) *kita/if,* (pl.) *katāfi* shoulder

kiya/er, (pls.) *kiye/ārāt* spoon

klāyasku ~ *klasku* (no pl.) girl of marriageable age

kobo kobo (100 kobo = 1 N)

kōfi coffee

kōkāb, (pl.) *kawākīb* harpoon

kolči groundnut(s)

komfani, -yāt company

koptani, -yāt kind of small gown

ko/ura electric light, electric socket, bulb, electricity

kōrak, bikōrak roar, bellow, shout, scream, shriek

kōrōkōrō type of thread; kind of game involving dancing

ko(ro)rāk roar, bellow, shout, scream, shriek (n.)

kōs, (pl.) *kīsān* small bowl

krēb grain used for making couscous

kri/allo (no pl.) small lizard

kū (f.), (d.) *-ʾēn,* (pl.) *-ʾān* forearm, elbow

kubbāret addār elite people

kubbārīye council of chiefs or rulers

kudāda exercise (n.)

kudub (no pl.) lie (n.)

kufā, (pl.) *kafāyi* parfleche

kufūfu buds of guinea corn

kuǰera, -āt chair, couch

kūká, (coll.) *kūk* kind of tree in bush

kulkulé, (coll.) *kúlkule* kind of large tree in bush

kulla whole; again, at all, even (adv.); anything
 ____ *(ke)* everything
 ____ *sawa (ley)* It's all the same!
 ____ *ši* everything

kull(i) any, every
 ____ *nādi/um* ~ *minē* (any)one, everyone
 ____ *še* anything
 ____ *yōm* everyday

kullu, ____ *nnās* all the people
 ____ *še* everything

kull(um) all

kulūfi, kulūfīye, -īn, -āt boastful

kūmāga Kumaga (Arab-speaking village in N.E. Nigeria, twenty miles from Fort-Lamy)

kumm, (d.) *-ēn,* (pls.) *kumme* ~ *kamāme/a* sleeve of a baba riga (big gown)

kundumá, (coll.) *kundum* hornless cow

kungo (no pl.) stick for knocking down fruit

kup handcuffs

ku/ora electric light

kūra soccer, football

kurbāǰ, (pl.) *karābīǰ* curved throwing knife

kurčīye, (coll.) *kurči* cucumber

kūre old(en)

kurkut old woman without hair

kursi, (pl.) *karasa* chair

kurtāl, (pl.) *karātīl azzāt* travel bag

kurúl, (pl.) *karala* serving spoon

kūsá, (coll.) *kūsa* (metal) nail; tin

kuskus couscous

kuškušá ~ *xušxušá,* (colls.) *kuškuš* ~ *xušxuš* *kindling wood*

kūzi, (pl.) *kawāzi* house, hut

kwayyis, kwayse, -īn, -āt nice
___ *bilēn* fantastic

L

l- towards

la- in order to

lā no

laban milk (n.)

labax, bulbux (*fōg*) set (tr.)

labbad, bilabbid hide (tr.)

labbas, bilabbis wear, dress (tr.)

lābile, -yāt curtain

lābis, -īn well-dressed (of men)

labudda certainly, definitely

lād, bulūd (*wara*) *albēt* go to the toilet

ladab etiquette, (good) manners

ladān, -īn muezzin

lādīye, (pl.) *ladāy*(*e*) clay cooker, fireplace, kitchen

lafat, bilfit turn toward s.o.
 ____ *rāsa* turn one's head

laffa, bilaffa cover
 ____, *bilaffi* fold
 ____, *buluff* wind, tie around; be angry or mad

laffat, bilaffit turn around

laftān hospital

laga, bilga arrive
 ____ *ʾassāʾa* be lucky

lāga, bilāgi meet

lagam, bilgam put food in one's mouth

laggaṭ, bilaggiṭ collect, pick (fruit)

laha, bilhi strip a tree of its bark

lāhag, bilāhig reach an outcome

lahamá indigestion

lahas, bilhas scoop

lahat, bilhat notice, perceive

lahhaǰ, bilahhiǰ bring

lahhan, bilahhin chastise

lahhās, -āt index finger

laʾāda commission (middle man's percentage)

laʾan, bilʾan curse

lāǰá, (coll.) *lāǰa* large tortoise

lakab (sg./pl.) nickname

lāki few, little [for mass nouns only]

lakka, bulukk mix, stir
 ____ (*bil fangame*) kick (with spurs)

lālé ~ *lālēk, -i, -u, -an* Greetings!/Well done!

lām, bulūm blame

lama, bilma collect; blend

lāmá, (coll.) *laham* meat
 laham axaḍar fresh meat
 laham mašwi roasted meat

lamba mark (n.)

lamlam, bilamlim collect together, gather (tr.)

lamma, -āt crowd (n.)
 ____ *-t annās* crowd

lamma, bulumm, ____ (*l-*) collect, gather together, meet, get together
 ____ *lxēl* race horses
 ____ *māl* save money
 ____ *rāsa* plan, intend; cooperate

lammas, bilammis touch (v.)

lamsān touch (n.)

lān, bulūn be soggy

langat, bilangit close

lantarki (no pl.) electric light, bulb, (electric) socket, electricity

laqam, (pl.) *luqumme* gum (anat.)

laqan (sg./pl.) nickname

lawa, bilwi bend (tr.)

lawān, -āt district head

lawiya (no pl.) lawyer

lawwa, bilawwi twist

lawwan, bilawwin dye

lāxirīn, lāxirāt other

lazam bilzam know well
 ____, *bulzum* stay

lazza, bilizz push, shove, bump into
 ____ *alwatīr* drive a car
 ____ *ddarb* put up a barricade

le road

l(e)- ~ *la-* for, to; have, possess

lēgos Lagos

lēlé, (coll.) *lēl,* (pl.) *layāli* night

lēmūn orange (color)

lēmūná, (coll.) *lēmūn* (*annaṣāra*) lemon, orange

lešinu why?

lētir lighter (n.)

(*li l*)*hallāka* Danger!

li/ubās clothes

li/ubb(*a*) center, midst of

libis, bilbas put clothes on, wear

li/ubtān hospital

lībyá, (coll.) *lībya* bean

līf (no pl.) holiday, vacation

ligdir bucket, pail, bottle

ligi, bilga receive, get, reach, find, earn, succeed
 ____ *l'āfi* recover, regain one's health

ligiya He found it.

līhe bark (bot.)

lihig, bilag reach, meet

lihik, bilhak be enough, suffice

lihis taste (n.)
 ____, *bilas* lick, taste, touch

li'ib dance, dancing, parade
 ____, *bil'ab* dance, play (v.)

lijām, (pl.) *lujumme* bit of a bridle, rein

liktāy doctor

limis ~ *lamas, bilmas* touch

l/fin sub(*b*)*āṯ* because

lisān, (pl.) *lisinne* tongue, speech, language

lissa yet

lō, (pls.) *līh/yān* (writing) tablet, blackboard
 ____ *alkitif* shoulder blade

lōda car horn

lōm blame (n.)

lōn, (pl.) *alwān* color

lu/ibb(*a*) center, midst of
 ____ *allēl* midnight, 12:00 to 4:00 A.M.
 ____ *arrijil* sole (of foot)
 ____ *lbēt,* (pl.) ____ *lbiyūt* floor
 ____ *lhille* center of town

lubbāni, lubbānīye, -īn, -āt middle

lug(*u*)*má,* (d.) *lugumtēn,* (pls.) *li/ugām* handful, mouthful

lūlū (sg./pl.) pearl

lumma lxēl horse race

luqa, -āt language, speech

luwāli marriage guardian

M

mā/i ~ *mu* not (negative copula), non-, un-
___/*lā* + impf. Don't . . . !
___ *badri ʾintāri ʾinta jīt* I don't know if it is you who has come.
___ *b/nagdar nugušša* I'm not able to broom it, (i.e., sweep it).
___ *baʾagla* unintentionally
___ *baʾāwin haw ma baṭīk māl čat* I won't help and I won't give you money either.
___ *bamši kam mā mašēt* ~ ___ *bamši se kan ʾinta timíš* I won't go unless you go as well.
___ *bērif grā mā bērif kitāb* illiterate
___ *bidri* unintentionally
___ *bisma lkalām* misbehave
___ *biziyāda ma fi nakisān* no more, no less
___ *fi* there is not; already
___ *fi niʾis* He is already asleep.
___ *fi še* unintentionally; Never mind./It doesn't matter.
___ *fi še beqallib alla* There is nothing above God.
___ *gaʾad ṭawwal* He didn't stay for long.
___ *gāsi* simple, easy
___ *gawi* not strong
___ *ʾadīl/ʾādil/ʾadilān* unjust
___ *ʾārif še* uncivilized (person)
___ *ʾāwur* innocent, not guilty
___ *ʾinda fāyde/fāydāt* useless
___ *ʾinda hāja fi xidimta* He neglected his work.
___ *ʾinda manfaʾa/manāfi* useless
___ *ʾinda sāʾa* He is unfortunate.
___ *ʾindi/ley hāja* I don't care.
___ *kalkal* not quite (so), not alright, untrue, incorrect
___ *kātib* illiterate
___ *labudda* unnecessary
___ *le-* than (comparative)
___ *mašēt layarwa dugō* I haven't gone to Maiduguri yet.
___ *mihimm, -a, -īn, -āt* unimportant
___ *nāfi* (all genders/numbers) useless
___ *niye* unintentionally
___ *rāda* It's all the same!
___ *sahī* untrue, incorrect
___ *simī lkalām* misbehave
___ *šaba* different
___/*lā tišrab* Don't drink!
___ *wājib* inappropriate, unnecessary
___ *yābis* not dry
___ *zēn, -e, -īn, -āt* no(t) good

mabarad, (pl.) *mabārīd* straight iron bar for digging holes

mablūl, -a, -īn, -āt damp, wet

mablūm, -a, -īn, -āt stupid, retarded, idiot(ic)

mabni, -ye, mabinyīn, mabinyāt built

mabsūṭ, -a, -īn, -āt happy

mabtūr, -a, -īn, -āt loose

mabxar, (pl.) *mabāxir* bowl for heating and burning perfume

madagg, (pl.) *mudugge* mud bin for storing guinea corn

madām, -āt round mud hut with grass roof

madax, bundux chew; eat guinea corn or vegetables

madda, bimidd measure

maddax, bimaddix chew

madfūn, -a, -īn, -āt corpse

madhak funny

madīde, (pl.) *madāyid* gruel of millet or rice with milk; local beer, alcoholic beverage (term used by drinkers)

madrasa, (pl.) *madāris* school

madyūn, -a, -īn, -āt borrower

(*ma*)*ḍīfe* act of being a guest

maḍmūn, -a, -īn, -āt borrower

maḍyūf, -īn host
 ____ *-a, -āt* hostess

mafhūm, -a, -īn, -āt understood

mafilso Mafilso (Arabic-speaking town in N.W. Cameroun)

mafindi, -īye, mafandi, mafindīyāt very strong

ma/ifrak, (pl.) *mafārik* screwdriver

mafsal, (pl.) *mafāsil* joint (anat.)
 ____ *alʾīd* wrist
 ____ *alkaʾab* ankle

maftū(h) open (adj.)

māfwá ~ *māfōyá,* (pl.) *māfu* stalk of sweet guinea corn

māga, bimāgi beg, implore, importune

magaǰi, (pl.) *-yīn* older brother

magaǰīye, -āt older sister

magass scissors

magatt life, living

magdūd, -a, -migaddadīn, -āt holey

maggan, bimaggin plant (a tree)

maggās, -īn boatman, pole for pushing a boat

magīl place in which one spends the daytime

magirá, -āt head woman, chairwoman

magli, -ye, -yīn, -yāt fried

mahabūb, -a, -īn, -āt beloved, loved one

mahabūs, -a, -īn, -āt trapped (inside), prisoner

mahaǰam, (pl.) *mahāǰim* cow horn used in scarifying and cupping

mahāǰiri ~ *mihāǰir,* (pls.) *ma/ihāǰirīn* beggar who habitually studies Koran

mahall, -āt place (n.)

mahalūb, -a, -īn, -āt stupid

mahama sandy country

maharūt, -e, -īn, -āt cultivated

mah/xaṭṭ, -āt storage place
 ____ *ʾalme* olla, communal water source

mahawagá, -āt fence

mahawūǰ, -a, -īn, -āt poor, needy

maʾa with

maʾadūr, -a, -īn, -āt injured

maʾakil livelihood, living

maʾarūf, -a/e, -īn, -āt known, common

maʾāwaga, -āt (*fōg addarb*) (car) accident

maʾāwana help (n.)

maʾrūf, -a, -īn, -āt well-known

maʾsūr, -e, -īn, -āt wanting s.t. very much

māʾūn, (pl.) *mawāʾīn* container, receptacle, dish, plate

maǰalis, (pl.) *maǰālis* committee, council

maǰannas, -a, -īn, -āt multi-colored (inanim.), dirty; argumentative, habitually disagreeing (person)

maǰnūn, -a, -īn, -āt crazy

maǰra ʾalme brook

māk, (d.) *-ēn* eyelid

makabarak, -i, -u, -an Greetings!

makaranta ~ *makarantīye, -āt* school

makhāla, -āt container for eye cosmetics

(m)ākil, -e, -īn, -āt eaten, eating

makka, bumukk pass through

maklūf, -a, -īn, -āt adult, mature, post-puberty

makmak, bimakmik stammer

makmāk, -a, -īn, -āt stammering

maknūs, -a/e, -īn, -āt bad, no(t) good, useless, naughty, dirty

makrū, -ha, -hīn, -hāt disliked, hated

maksab (no pl.) profit

maksūr, -a, -īn, -āt broken

makšū(h), makšūha, -īn, -āt uncovered, open

maktaʾa, -āt next to, (on the other) side (of)

maktūb, (pls.) *-āt* ~ *makātīb* book, magazine, letter

maktūl killed

makwā, (pl.) *-t* (branding, flat) iron

māl, (pls.) *amwāl* ~ *mīlān* money, fund, loan property
 ___ *abyaḍ* silver money
 ___ *almaǰūb* dowry

māl, bimīl (*min*) be balanced

mala, bimli be filled; wind

māla/malā (*ke*) why?

malafāyá, (pl.) *malāfi* big mat

malak, bimlik govern, rule, possess, own

malāk, (pl.) *malāyik* angel

mālak, mālki, -u, -an What's the matter?

mālam, -īn learned (person in Islam)

malamm, -āt gathering, meeting

malaṭ, bum(*u*)*luṭ* uproot

malax, bumlux pull

malbūs (no pl.) old clothes, hand-me-down(s)

malēš What's wrong?

malik, (pl.) *mulūk* king
 ___ *-e,* (pl.) *malkāt* queen

mālik, -e, -mālkīn, -āt owner

mal(ʾ)*ān, -a, -īn, -āt* full, crowded

mallas, bimallis polish

mallaṭ, bimalliṭ pluck or pick (weeds or grass)

malwi, malwīye, malwīn, malwāt twisted

mambará, (pl.) *mambar* stair(s)

mamlūs, -e, -īn, -āt polished

mamša (no pl.) transport(ing)
 ___ *balʾagil ma bitar almuwāṣil* Slowness does not prevent arrival.

mān- + suff. (negative copula)
 ___ *-i ʾārif sināʾa wāhade kulla* I don't know a single trade at all.
 ___ *-i raḍyān/rāḍi* I don't agree.
 ___ *-i xābir še* I don't have any news.

mana, bimna show that one has power

manāhaǰa being out of breath

manfaʾa, (pl.) *manāfi* use(fulness), advantage, benefit

mangalo (no pl.) mango

māni ~ *manī, -ʾe, -ʾīn, -ʾāt* powerful, strong, big and strong

manša, (pl.) *mamāši* journey

maqabbiš, -e, -īn, -āt pale beige

maqīb west

maqšūš, -a, -īn, -āt cheated or swindled one

mara, (pls.) *nasāwīn* ~ *awīn* ~ *maray* ~ *mrē* ~ *mrāt* woman, wife

maraba Welcome!

marab(*āy*)*á,* (pls.) *marābi*(*yāt*) shirt

marā/ūd desire, wish, aim, goal, liking, love

maraḍ disease, sickness

marag, bumrug bring s.t. out

maragá (no pl.) broth, meat soup

marak, bumruk come out

ma/irāka, (pl.) *marāyik* grindstone

maras, bumurus massage

marbaṭ, (pl.) *marābiṭ* anything worn around the neck

marbūṭ, -a, -īn, -āt tied, bound, prisoner

mardu kind of tree or fruit thereof

marḍān, -a, -īn, -āt ill, sick

marfaʾīn iron handle for fetching a water bucket

marfāʾīn, marfaʾīne, (pl.) *marāfiʾīn* hyena

marfak, (d.) *-ēn,* (pl.) *marāfik* elbow

margadá width

marhūm, -a, -īn, -āt deceased, the late . . .

marʾūb, -a, -īn, -āt coward

marī fertile, rich (of soil)

marīḍ, -e, -īn, -āt, ill, sick

mārin, mārne, (pl.) *murun* fine, soft, smooth

marīse, (pl.) *marāyis* alcoholic beverage, local brew, beer *markaba,* (pl.) *marākib* canoe, boat, ship

markūb(á), (pl.) *marākīb* sandal, shoe

marra, -āt instance, occasion, time
___ *wāhade* once
___ *-āt katīrāt* frequently, often
___ *-tēn* twice

marraḍ, bimarriḍ make s.o. sick

marrag, bimarrig drive out

marsūl, -a, (pl.) *marāsīl* messenger

martaba, (pl.) *marātīb* authority, power, influence; position, situation

marte Marte (village 45 miles northeast of Maiduguri, in N.E. Nigeria)

maryūd, -a, -īn, -āt beloved, loved, lovely

mās, bumūs melt

masa, bimsa rub, clean, paint

masak, bumsuk hold, take hold of
___ *dīna* adhere to one's religion

masalan for example

masamman particularly

masar maize, (Indian) corn

masātir graveyard (pl. of *mastará*)

māsax, māsxe, -īn, -āt tasteless, bland, plain, unseasoned, unsalted, sugarless; infertile

masāxa insult (n.)

masdūd, -e, -īn, -āt blocked, obstructed, closed

mashūr, -a, -īn, -āt hexed (as a result of the 'evil eye', usually cast by women)

masī, -ʾe, -ʾīn, -ʾāt vagabond

masíč, (pl.) *masāyič* mosque

masīl, (pl.) *masāyil* stream

masǰūn, -a, -īn, -āt prisoner

maskana poverty

masmas, bimasmis rinse
___ *gaddūma* He rinsed out his mouth.
___, ___ *xumāma* wash clothes

masra grazing

mas(s)a, bimiss touch, kiss

massās, -a, -īn, -āt cannibal

mas(s)ax, bumsux insult, curse

mastahī, -ye, mastahīn, -āt sensible

mastará, (pl.) *masātir* grave

maša, bim/nši (l-) go, walk

mašābik tree trunk

mašēt going (n.)
___ *-i hīl fōtiskum* my going (journey) to Potiskum

māši, māšye, māšīn, -āt going (act. part.)
___ *wa* Will you go?
___ *-īn se* Shall we [inclusive] go?

mašqūl, -a, -īn, -āt busy

mašša, bimišš clean, erase

maššāš, -āt eraser

maššaṭ, bimaššiṭ braid (hair)

maššāṭa, -āt hairdresser

maššāy, -a, -īn, -āt s.o. who walks quickly

mašūr, -a, -īn, -āt famous

māt, bumūt die, be extinguished

matá when?

matarāra, -āt spindle

mātir, -e, -īn, -āt far [but less so than *baʾīd*]

matti borrowed seed guinea corn

maṭara storm

maṭarak, (pl.) *maṭārik* small tree branch, stick for building a house

maṭṭa, bumuṭṭ extend

mawrūd, -a, -īn, -āt suffering from an illness

māwūǰ, -e, -īn, -āt curved

maxanūg, -a, -īn, -āt eclipsed

maxarūga, (pls.) *maxārig* ~ *maxarūgāt* hip

maxaṭar, (pl.) *maxāṭir* journey

maxaṭūṭ, -a, -īn, -āt placed in a particular location

maxazan dispensary, storeroom

maxēt kind of tree or fruit thereof

maxsūs, -a, -īn, -āt special

mayyit, mayte, maytīn, -āt dead (one)

maznūb, -e, -īn, -āt guilty

meʾellem, (pl.) *meʾelmīn* (male) teacher of Islamic subjects, usually Koran

mēl mail

mēre red guinea corn

meskīn, (pl.) *maskana* poor person destined to remain so

mētam almōt funeral ceremony

miä̆ not (negative copula), non-, un-

mibāʾa buy(ing) (n.)

mibarsā confidence

midabbib, -īn hunchback

midakkin, -e, -īn, -āt dark- or dull-colored (generally dark brown)

midarese, -āt female teacher

midd, (d.) *-ēn* measurement for selling (by calabash)

midda sātak fi še You don't care about anything!

midda sāti I don't care.

migallam -a, -īn, -āt leper

migdār quantity, size

mihāǰir, -īn young adult male of approximately 25 years

mihāmi, -ye, -īn, -āt helper, assistant

mihanhana neigh(ing)

mihimm, -a, -īn, -āt important, urgent, serious

miʾaddil, -e, -īn, -āt repaired

mīl (sg./pl.) mile

milāga (no pl.) meeting

milhakkir, -e, -īn, -āt cross-legged

milharib, milharbe, -īn, -āt enemy, adversary

milhazzime, -āt well-dressed (of women)

milʾammil, -e, -īn, -āt ready

mili/eh ~ *milhe* ~ *milē* salt
 ___ *kikiye* kind of salt

milkanǰir, -īn hunchback

millāsif, -a, -īn, -āt bright (of light)

millawlu, -we, -wīn, -wāt twisted, crooked

milwayyid, -e, -īn, -āt depending only on God; third (ring) finger

milye/ōn, (pl.) *malāyīn* million

mimattir, -e, -īn, -āt far (of people)

mi/un from, of; including; when, since (conj.); than (comparative)
 ___ *assabāh* in the morning
 ___ *ayyōm liyā giddām* from now on
 (___) *gabul* before, formerly, previously
 ___ *hinē yā giddām* from now on
 ___ *ǰāy yā giddām* in the future
 (___) *ṭaw(w)a* before, formerly, previously

mi/andīl, (pl.) *manādīl* (hand)kerchief, woman's scarf or hair wrap

minē who(se)?, whom?
 ___ *habbāb arradio da* To whom does this radio belong?
 ___ *kulla* whoever, everyone

mingāš, (pl.) *manāgīš* pin

minǰamm, -a, -īn, -āt (at) ease, relaxed, comfortable

minmatt, -e, -īn, -āt horizontal

minnasabah 6:00 A.M. to 8:00 A.M.

minti mint, candy

miriḍ ~ *muruḍ* ~ *mariḍ, bumruḍ* be sick

mirsāl sending

misadda revenge

misanni, -ye, -yīn, -yāt expecting, waiting

misēmīr, (pl.) *misēmirāt* small nail

misil like, as, similar to
 ___, (pl.) *misāl* example
 ___ *da* for example; same thing
 ___ *ke* thus
 ___ *tumūt dugō* as if she nearly died
 ___ *ṭaw(w)a* as (like) before

miskīn, (pl.) *masākīn* poor man

mismār, (pl.) *masāmir* (metal) nail

misōʾar, -a, -īn, -āt mad (of dogs only)

mišakkik, -e, -īn, -āt doubtful

mišaqala (no pl.) interruption

mišehid, -īn righteous man

mišingāri, (pl.) *mišingārīn* hunter

mišōṭin, -a, -īn, -āt crazy, mad, violent

mi/uš(š)āṭ braid(s)

mitwaffi, -ye, mitwaffīn, -āt dead, deceased

miṭawwil ~ *muṭawwal* (long) ago, a long time ago

mixaddir, -e, -īn, -āt greenish, tarnished

miyaqqin, -a, -īn, -āt certain, sure

miye (*wāhade*) (one) hundred

miytēn two hundred

mizaffir, -e, -īn, -āt fetid, putrid

mīzān (no pl.) scale (for weighing)

mīzé, (pl.) *mīze* nanny goat

mizrāg, (pl.) *mazārig* wood for making spears

mobilet motorcycle

mōdi, mōdīye, -yīn, -yāt wicked

mōgad annār fireplace

mongo (no pl.) small monkey

mōt death

moxola ~ *muxla,* (pl.) *maxāli* handbag, suitcase

mu/i negative copula

mubanna built

mudabbir, -e, -īn, -āt clever, hard-working

mudaffa, -ye, -mudaffīn, -āt cooked

mudarris, (pls.) *mu/idarsīn* (male) teacher of Islamic subjects, usually Koran

mudāwará, -āt fence

mudawwam, -e, -īn, -āt permanent

mudayyig, mudayyge, -īn, -āt worried

mudugāgá, (pls.) *mi/adāgīg* hammer, stick for pounding grain

muḍārar, -īn polygamist

muḍawwi, -ye, -yīn, -yāt illuminated

muḍurri, -ye, -īn, -āt cheater, criminal

mufatti, -ye, -yīn, -yāt awake

mufrāg, (pl.) *mafārīg* hot piece of wood used for ritual scarification of the forehead, stomach or back of the neck; ritual scar on forehead

mu/iftā(h), (pl.) *mafātī* key

mugābala interview

mug/qābil, -e, -īn, -āt across, opposite (direction), facing

mugaddar, -a, -īn, -āt impulsive

mugargar, -a, -īn, -āt hollow

mugāwala (no pl.) rumor

mugušāšá, (pl.) *-āt* broom

muhawwag, -e, -īn, -āt (*b-*) surrounded (by or with)

muʾaddab, -a, -īn, -āt cultured, polite

muǰaddar, -a, -īn, -āt s.o. who has chicken pox

mukarfas, -e, -īn, -āt wrinkled

mu/ikarram, -e, -īn, -āt cannibal, witch

mukaršam, -e, -īn, -āt wrinkled

mukassar, -a, -īn, -āt cripple

mukawwas, -a, -īn, -āt chewed

mukulli, (pl.) *-yāt* key

m/yumkin possible, possibly, perhaps, maybe

munāfix, munāfx/qe, -īn, -āt hypocrite, rascal

munāfqa hypocrisy

munxur ~ *muxurr,* (pl.) *muxurre* nose

muqabbin, -i, -īn, -āt sad

muqrāfá, -āt calabash spoon used for taking cooked guinea corn from the pot

muq/ɣru/ib sunset, evening, 6:00 P.M. to 8:00 P.M.; evening prayer

mura/ubba, (pl.) *-ʾāt* square

murabba, murabbiye, murabbīn, -āt adopted child

murr, -a, -īn, -āt bitter, sour; sad(ness), misery, objection
____ *-ak fīni šinu* What can I do for you?
____ *-ak šinu* What business is it of yours?

mūs, (pl.) *mawasa* razor, shaving knife

mūsa Moses

musāǰil, -e, -īn, -āt urgent

musannam, -a, -īn, -āt superstitious

musrān, (pls.) *masār*(īn) intestine

musulmāy ~ *musi/ulum, musulmātiye, musulmīn, -āt* Muslim

muṣībe ~ *nasībe,* (pl.) *masāyib* misfortune

mušāwara, -āt consultation, discussion

mutabbit, -e, -īn, -āt certain, sure

muta'ālim, muta'ālme, -īn, -āt educated

muṭaffil, -e, -īn, -āt senile

muṭahhir, -e, -īn, -āt circumcised

muṭallag, -a, -īn, -āt divorced

muṭarṭar, -a, -īn, -āt fat (adj.)

muṭāwil, -e, -īn, -āt horizontal

muṭawwal ~ *miṭawwil* long ago

muṭayyir, muṭayyre, -īn, -āt witch, wizard

muwakkit, -e, -īn, -āt certain, sure

muwāli, -ye, -muwālīn, -āt near

muwaqqir, -e, -īn, -āt perspiring, sweating

muxālif, muxālfa, -īn, -āt against

muxawwaf, -e, -īn, -āt fearful

muxla ~ *moxola,* (pl.) *maxāli* handbag, suitcase

muxx brain

N

nabagá, (coll.) *nabag* kind of fruit

nabah, bimba bark (v.)

nabāt (no pl.) plant

nabī, (pl.) *nuba* prophet

nada moisture

nāda, bināḍi call s.o.

nadāma regret (n.)

nādar, (pl.) *nawādir* temple (anat.)

nādarat, tinādir behave like a harlot, go whoring

naddab, binaddib flatter, praise

nādi/um, (pl.) *nās* person, client; (pl.) people [Cf. also under *nās*]
___ *hāmi* hard worker
___ *hana* native of

naḍāfa cleanliness

naḍḍaf, binaḍḍif clean (v.)

naḍḍārāt glasses

naḍīf, -e, -īn, -āt clean, pretty, beautiful, nice, fantastic

nafa, bi/unfa help, be useful (for)

nāfa, bināfi benefit

nafadá, (pl.) *nafad* pimple, sore

nafar, -āt tribe; kind, type
___ *da* same thing; like this

nafas breath
___, *binfas* give birth, bring forth

nafaš, bin/mfiš comb or brush one's hair

nafax, bunfux breathe or blow out, exhale, extinguish; feed

naffad, binaffid winnow

naffal, binaffil pray (not compulsory)

naffas, binaffis breathe

naffāsa, -āt midwife

naffāš, -āt comb (n.)

naffāxa, -āt bellows

nāfi, -ye, -yīn, -yāt useful

nafis evil eye

nafīza, -āt window

nafnif, -e, -īn, -āt moist, soggy, soft

nafs (f.), (pl.) *nufūs* soul, -self (in reflexives)
___ *-a* himself, itself (m.)
___ *-aha* herself, itself (f.)
___ *-ak, nafski, -ku, -kan* yourself, yourselves
___ *-ana* ourselves
___ *-i* myself

nafulá, -āt prayer (not compulsory)

nāga, -āt barren land

nāgá, -āt she-camel

naga'a (no pl.) clearing (of land), cleared plot of land, cracked soil (due to drought)

nagal, bungul remove, transport

nagan, bunugun sniff (of animals)

nagas, bungus (*attaman*) reduce (price)

nagāsa (no pl.) reduction

nagaṭá, (coll.) *nagaṭ* drop (of liquid)

nagga, binaggi peel

naggaṭ, binaggiṭ fall, drip
___ *-at* (pl.) *naggaṭ 'alme* waterfall

nāgis, -e, -īn, -āt deficient

nahaḍ, binhaḍ go to war with

nahār, (pls.) *-āt* ~ *nuhurre* daytime

nahīḍ war

nahīf, -e, -īn, -āt malnourished, emaciated

nahīs, -e, -īn, -āt troublemaker, vicious, evil (person)

na'am yes (when being called)

na'āmá, (coll.) *na'ām,* (pl.) *nu'umme* ostrich

na/i'ās ~ *niyās* rest, sleep (n.)

naira, -āt naira (₦ = approximately $1.55 during 1973-1974)

naǰa, binǰu escape

naǰā success
  ___, *binǰa* succeed

nāǰá, -āt ewe

naǰar, bunǰur carve

naǰas, binǰas move one's bowels

naǰāsa filth

naǰid, -e, -īn, -āt clever, experienced; not ripe, green

nāǰid, -e, -īn, -āt ripe; cunning

naǰimá, (pl.) *nujūm* star

naǰǰad, binaǰǰid cook or prepare food

naǰǰār kind of tool
  ___ *(aššadar)* ~ *naǰǰāri,* (pl.) *naǰǰārīn (aššadar)* carpenter

naǰǰas, binaǰǰis move one's bowels

nāk, binīk have sexual intercourse

naka, binka (*l-* or d.o.) get married, marry

nakar, bunkur deny, object

nakat, bunkut dig a hole or well

nākir, -e, -īn, -āt stubborn

nākirān, -a, -īn, -āt stubborn

nākiya (no pl.) cake baked with honey

nāl very tall grass in the bush

nālá, (coll.) *nāla* bee

nām, binām ~ *bunūm* sleep

namba (no pl.) number

nami/ulá, (coll.) *namil* ant (usually black)

namma, binamma slander

nammāy, -a, -īn, -āt slanderer

nammūsá ~ *nāmūsá* ~ *namsá,* (coll.) *nāmūs* mosquito

nāmūsīye, -āt mosquito net

nāna mint (bot.)

nāna, -yāt king's wife (any of the four)

naqaṣ, bunquṣ lack

nār (f.), (pl.) *nīrān* fire, lighter
  ___ *alwāyar* electric light, electricity

nās people (pl. of *nādi/um*)
  ___ *abdīn/karīmīn* benevolent people
  ___ *katīrīn* many people
  ___ *wādāt* some people (f.)
  ___ *wādīn* some people (m.)

nās, bunūs whimper, yelp (of dogs only)

nasa, binsa advise

nasar, binisir conquer, succeed

nasara victory, success

nasīb, -a, (pls.) *nus(u)bāna* in-law
  ___, (pl.) *nasāyib* father-in-law
  ___, *-e* (pl.) *nasāyib* mother-in-law

nasīb fate, fortune
  ___ *-e* ~ *muṣībe,* (pl.) *masāyib* misfortune

nasī(h), nisīhe, -īn, nasyāt healthy, well

nasīhe advice

nasīle, (pl.) *nasāyil* splinter

nassa, binassi heal

nassa, bunuss roast on a spit

nassar, binassir be victorious

naṣi, bin/mṣa recover

naṣrāni ~ *naṣāri, naṣarīye, naṣāra, naṣārīyāt* Caucasian, white (person), Christian

nāšab, bināšib shoot

našad, binšid ask
  ___ *ley wēn ǰikkāta* He asked me where his bag is.

našāṭ energy

našīde demand, inquiry

našīṭ, -e, -īn, -āt energetic

našša, binišš search for pasture

naššab, binaššib shoot

naššāq, -a, -īn ~ *niššāqa, -āt* nomad

našū, (pl.) *nišā* boy of 15 to 20 years

natar, buntur (*fōg*) scold

naṭṭa, bunuṭṭ jump

nawa, binwa intend

naxaš, bunxuš scratch

na(y)'al, binal ~ *bine'il* curse

nāyir, nāyre, -īn, -āt bright (-colored)

nayy, -e, -īn, -āt not well-cooked, not ripe

nayyal, binayyil dye

nazal, binzil descend, climb

nazar, bunzur glance

nazūla arrival

nazzal, binazzil help s.o. climb down; put s.o. up for a few days, shelter, house

nifāsa, -āt childbirth

ni/a'āla, (pl.) *ni'ille* shoe

ni'īma fertility, prosperity

ni'is, binas sleep

nijayyid, nijayyde, -īn, -āt clever, experienced

najid, binjid ripen

ni/ajid, -e, -īn, -āt cooked, prepared; clever, experienced

nijis dung, dirt(y), filth(y)

nīle indigo

nimir, (pl.) *numurre* leopard

nī/esān, -a, -īn, -āt drowsy, sleepy, sleeping, asleep

nisī, binsa forget
 ___ *-t* (*aššey*) *algāla* I forgot what he said.

nisyān, -a, -īn, -āt forgetful

nišābá, (pl.) *nišāb* arrow

nišde, -āt question

nišīf fi darbak sā'a talāta We are expecting you at three o'clock.

niyās ~ *ni/a'ās* asleep, rest (n.)

niye intention(ally)

nizil, binzil arrive

nōm rest, sleep (n.)

nuggārá, (pl.) *nagāgīr* big drum

nugra, (pl.) *nugār* hole

nukā marriage
 be ___ + pron. suff. married

nukur (no pl.) denial

nūr algamar moonlight

nuss, (pl.) *nasasa* half
 ___ *allēl* midnight
 ___ *alyōm/alharrā* half a day
 ___ *annahār* midday
 ___ *issā'a* half an hour
 ___ *-e sana* half a year

nusur victory

Ñ

ñamñamīye long drizzle (during July-August)

ñaññāgá, -āt drizzle (n.)

ñarra, buñurr purr

ñāwa, -āt cat

O

ōgad, bi'ōgid ~ bi'ogd (annār) light or build a fire

ōlag, bi'ōlig light a fire

ora, bo'ori tell

ōra, -āt wrong (n.)

ōra, bi'ōra mention

ōra ley Tell me!/Show me!

ōrá one-eyed woman

orakku 'āfi I hope you (m.pl.) are well.

orekkan āfi I hope you (f.pl.) are well.

orekki 'āfi I hope you (f.sg.) are well.

orētak āfi I hope you (m.sg.) are well.

orna Tell us!/Show us!

Q

qāb, biqīb disappear

qabban, biqabbin become angry

qabinān, -a, -īn, -āt sad

qabir, (pl.) *qubūr* grave

qada breakfast, lunch

qadar, biqadar cheat, swindle

qadda, biqaddi have breakfast or lunch (together)

qaddar, biqaddi/ar cheat, swindle

qaddēna sawa We had breakfast/lunch together.

qādi (*ke*) next time; (over) there

qaḍabān, -a, -īn, -āt angry

qafa, biqifi doze (off)

qaffal, biqaffil catch s.o. by surprise, ambush

qafiyān, -a, -īn, -āt dozing (off)

qaflān, -a, -īn, -āt drowsy, unaware

qalab, biqalab conquer, overcome

(*q*)*alam,* (pls.) *qulumma/e* ~ *qulūm* ~ *qulmān* pen

(*q*)*albān, -a, -īn, -āt* tired; pregnant

qāli, -ye, -yīn, -yāt expensive, high (in price)

qālib, qālbe, -īn, -āt victorious

qalīd, -e, -īn, -āt, (comm. pl.) *qulād* big, fat, obese (person), thick
 ____ *min* thicker

qalla guinea corn
 ____ *bēḍa* white guinea corn
 ____ *dāmirge* guinea corn soaked and dried

qamāmá, (coll.) *qamām* cloud

qamaz, buqmuz wink

qamīm, -e, -īn, -āt cloudy

qammaḍ, biqammiḍ, ____ *ʾēna* close one's eyes
 ____ *ʾīda* make a fist

qān, buqūn be angry

qanam(*āy*)*á,* (coll.) *qanam* goat, sheep, (small) livestock

qani, qanīye, -yīn, -yāt wealthy

qanna, biqanni sing

qannāy, -a, -īn, -āt singer

qār, buqūr ~ *biqīr* attack, plunder, raid

qara/ib, buqrub approach, capture, catch, (take) hold (of), overcome; acknowledge

qarāb, (pl.) *qurbān* crow, raven

qarad intention

qarād, (pl.) *qurūd* s.t. wanted or desired

qaraf, biqaraf (*almarkaba*) row (a boat)

qarazat, tuqruz wean

qarīb, -e, -īn, -āt west; foreign(er) [from another country]; alone

qarqara, baqarqir gargle

qarqarat, tiqarqir lactate, give milk

qarrāf(*á*), *-āt* oar; communal drinking cup always kept in the olla

qarya, -āt principal town

qasab, biqasab force (v.)

qasībe force (n.)

qassad, biqassid, ____ (*b-*) believe (in)
 ____ (*fōg/bēn*) agree (on)

(*q*)*assal, biq/ʾassil* wash (tr.)

qašim, (pls.) *qušūm* ~ *qušumme* mouth (outer portion), edge
 ____ *addarb/albāb/albēt* doorway
 ____ *albahar* riverbank

___ *albarrād* teapot spout
___ *assēf* sword tip
___ *assakkīn* knife tip
___ *aṭṭērá* bird's beak
___ *benna ʾarab* Our tribe is Arab.
___ *benna wāhid* We are related.
___ *bēt* tribe
___ *wāhid* simultaneously, at once, immediately

qašš, buqušš cheat, swindle

qaššāš, -a, -īn, -āt cheater, swindler

qayta, (pl.) *qayāti* flute

qayya/e love (n.)

qayyad, biqayyid offend

q/ʾayyan, biq/ʾayyin make s.o. angry

qayyar, biqayyir change; set (sun)

qazalá, (coll.) *qazal,* (pl.) *qazāl(ā)* gazelle
___ *birda* (gazelle) fawn

qazza, buquzz build, erect, put up

qēd anger

qēn haze
___ *fī* It's hazy.

qibbēšé, (coll.) *qibbēš* kind of small tree

qiḍib, buquḍub be angry

qilbat, taɣalab be(come) pregnant

qilib, baqlab be incapable of doing s.t., be unable

qilib, biqilab be tired; be pregnant

qine riches, wealth

qinné, (pl.) *qinne* poem, song

qiwi, biqwi love

qubūr graveyard [pl. of *qabir*]

qūlá, (coll.) *qūl,* (pl.) *qawala* fool; ghoul

qulāṭ argument

qumza, -āt wink (n.)

qurrá, (pls.) *-āt* ~ *qurūr* whiteblaze, whiteface

qušš cheating, swindling (n.)

R

rāba buttermilk

rābá, -āt (drinking) cup, glass

rabanna qašimna/kalāmna nuktul kabīrna We conspired to kill our boss.

rabaṭ, birbuṭ (*fi* or d.o.) tie (up), bind, imprison
 ___ *kalām* conspire
 ___ *qašim* make an agreement, conspire

rabb Lord (God)
 ___ *al ʾālamīn* God (lit., 'Lord of the worlds')

rabba, birabbi care, take care of, earn a living; grow (tr.)

rabbaṭ, birabbiṭ load

rabda, -āt ostrich (lit., 'multi-colored')

rābi, -ye, rābīn, -yāt fourth (ordinal)

rābi Rabi (p.n.f.)

rābit, rabda, (pl.) *rubut* multi-colored (anim.)

rābiṭ, (pl.) *rubbāṭ addarb* robber

rabrāb, -āt grass sifting plate

rād, birīd like, love; arouse, awaken; plan, intend

radd, burudd turn back

radda, burudd return (intr.)

radio, -āt radio

raḍa ~ *riḍī, birḍa* agree on, be satisfied

rāḍi, -ye, rāḍīn, -āt satisfied

rafa, birfa lift, raise

rafāga friendship

raff, (pl.) *riffāf* quarter (of a city)
 ___ *assakkāra* drinker's quarter

raffag, biraffig accompany s.o.

rafīg, -e, (pl.) *rufugān* friend

ragaba, (pl.) *rugubba* neck

ragabt, (pl.) *rugubb al ʾīd* wrist

ragad, burgud lie (down), go to bed, sleep
 ___ *-tu ʾāfi* Did you sleep well?

ragaṭá, (pl.) *ragaṭ* spot

raggad, biraggid relax (tr.), make s.o. rest

raggās, -a, -īn, -āt dancer

rāgid, rāgde, -īn, -āt lying down, sleeping

ragras, biragris cry (lit., 'be filled with tears')

rāh, birū disappear
 ___, *birūh* get lost

rahad (no pl.) water hole

rahál bed decorations; wooden surface for cooking utensils

rahama pity (n.)

rahamān, -a, -īn, -āt merciful

rahhab, birahhib welcome s.o.

rahhaf, birahhif soften

rahhal, birahhil bring s.t. out

rahīf, -e, (pl.) *ruhāf* soft, tender

rahîm, -a, -īn, -āt beneficent

rāʾa, birāʾi look at

raʾi opinion

rāʾi, (pl.) *rāʾīn* herdsman
 ___ *ssijīn,* ___ *assijīn* prison guard
 ___ *lqanam,* ___ *alqanam* shepherd

raʾīs, (pls.) *ruʾāsa* ~ *russe* boss, overseer, chief, president
 ___ *hana dār* head of state

raʾīye flock (n.)

rája, birja come back, return

rajab eighth month (of Islamic lunar calendar)

rajaf, birjif shake (intr.), tremble

rajīl, -e, -īn, -āt brave

rājil, (ds.) *rijālen* ~ *rijāl tinēn,* (pl.) *rijāl* man, husband

rajja, birajja wait (for)

rakkab, birakkib cook or prepare food

rakkāba ~ *rikāba,* (pl.) *-āt* step

rakkaz, birakkiz (*fōg*) lean (on)

rakkāz, -īn scarecrow

rama, birmi throw (down); dictate; lay an egg

ramaḍān Ramadan (twelfth month of Islamic lunar calendar)

ramalá, (coll.) *ramal* sand

ramaš, birmaš wink

rango finely-ground guinea corn

raqabān, -a, -īn, -āt greedy person

rās, (pls.) *russe* ~ *rūse* head; -self (in reflexives)
- ___ + pron. suff. + *anfata* be civilized
- ___ *albēt* roof
- ___ *alqalam* tip of a pen
- ___ *qalīd* big head
- ___ *-a* himself, itself (m.)
- ___ *-a (ʾa)nkasa/(ʾa)nfata* civilized person
- ___ *-a gawi* He is stubborn.
- ___ *-a laffat, rāsa tuluff* be angry or mad
- ___ *-a maṭalūs* uncivilized person
- ___ *-a yābis* He is perverse.
- ___ *-aha* herself, itself (f.)
- ___ *-ak, rāski, -ku, -kan* yourself, yourselves
- ___ *-ana* ourselves
- ___ *-i* myself

rasam, bursum draw, sketch

rasan, bursun tie together (mostly of fish or guinea corn)

rāsjār ~ *rās ajjār* money, capital

rassa, buruss pile up, stack

rassal, birassil send, (be in) charge (of)

rassās, (pl) *arsāsa* bullet

rasūl, -īn apostle, God's messenger

rašād red powder used for medicine

rašaf, buršuf bribe

rašāš light rain (before rainy season)

rašāwa, (pl.) *-āt* bribe

rašīk light rain (before rainy season)

rašša, birišš spray water

raššaš, biraššiš spray water

ratab, burtub beat a child who does not cry afterwards

rātib, -e, -īn, -āt child who, if beaten, does not cry

rātib, (pl.) *ruttāb* powerful

rattab, birattib arrange

raṭan, burṭun speak a foreign language

raṭīn (no pl.) foreign language

rawa, birwa be content(ed), satisfied or full (of water)

rāwiye, -āt rain cloud

rawwah, birawwih go home

rawwāx, -a, -īn, -āt goer, wanderer, s.o. always on the move

rawyān, -a, -īn, -āt content (adj.)

rāx, bu/irūx go out
- ___ *ke* He went around there.

raxīṣ, raxīṣa, -īn, -āt cheap

rāy (no pl.) idea

rayni, raʾīni, raʾūni, raʾanni Look at me!

rāyqīn ke They walked around.

rayyaz, bireyyiz cure, heal

razax, birzux make s.o. rich

razmá, (no pl.) *razamāt* package

rēke sugar cane

rēza razor

rība/i (no pl.) profit

ribṭé, (pls.) *ri/ubāṭ* bundle, parcel, package
- ___ *habil annaʾāla* shoelace

riḍī ~ *raḍa, birḍa* agree (on), be satisfied
- ___ (*fi*) nurse, suckle

rifge accompaniment

riga/eyyig, rigayyge, -īn, -āt thin

rī(h) (f.), (pl.) *riāha* wind, air
rī bārde cold wind
___ *kabīre,* ___ *kubār* tornado
___ *naḍīfe* pure air
___ *qalīde* big wind

rihik, bir(h)ak grind up (guinea corn)

riʾib, birʾab be a coward

riʾif, birʾaf have a bloody nose

riǰi ~ *raǰa, birǰa* wait (for)

riǰil (f.), (ds.) *riǰlē* ~ *riǰilē tinēn,* (pl.) *riǰlēn* foot, paw
___ *albār* tributary (of river)
___ *-e,* (pl.) *riǰil* foot (measure); wheel
___ *-e sitte* six feet

rikāba ~ *rakkāba, -āt* step; (pl.) ladder

rikib, birkab climb
___ (*fōg*) ride

riqim ~ *raq/ham, birq/ham* pity (v.)

rīš luck

rišif (no pl.) bribe

rišš, (pls.) *rušše* ~ *rašaša* eyebrow

rizix, rizxa, (pl.) *ruzux* fortunate

rizz rice

rōba lower part
___ *hīl ʾašima ʾaṭṭāba* cigarette filter

rōg, (pl.) *rīgān* row, line (on paper), furrow
___ *assirwāl* seam (of trousers)

rubū (one-)fourth, quarter

rugād rest, sleep (n.)

rū(h) spirit, -self (in reflexives)
___ *-a* himself, itself (m.)
___ *-aha* herself, itself (f.)
___ *-ak, rūhik, rūkku, rūkkan* yourself, yourselves
___ *-ana* ourselves
___ *-i* myself

rukubá, -āt hut, stall
___ *-t assūg* market hut or stall

rukubá, (pl.) *rikab* knee

rukun, -āt corner

rumāš, (pl.) *rumūš* eyelash

rummāná, (coll.) *rummān* pomegranate

ruzux riches, wealth

S

sā, busū go (away), leave

sāb, bisīb harm

saba seven

sabā(h) morning, east

sabak, bisubuk precede

sabba, busubb put; pour

sabbab, bisabbib get diarrhea

sabbāra, (pl.) *-āt* flash

sābi, -ye, -sābīn, -yāt seventh

sabīb diarrhea, dysentery

sabiʾīn seventy

sābūná, (coll.) *sābūn* soap

sadaka alms (not compulsory)

sadāx dowry

sadda, bisidd(a) close; pay (tr.)
 ___ *ʾattār* take revenge

saddād, (pl.) *-āt almaktūb* bookcover

saddag, bisaddig (d.o. or *b-*) trust, believe (in), have faith (in); prove

sadīg, -īn boyfriend
 ___ *-e, -āt* girlfriend

sādix, sādxe, -īn, -āt honest, candid, truthful, telling the truth

safar, busfur travel away

sāfar, bisāfir travel away

safarōg, (pl.) *safārīg* boomerang

saffa, bisaffi spill (tr.)

saffá, (d.) *saffitēn,* (pl.) *-āt* handful of uncooked (guinea) corn

saffāy, -āt strainer (usually for tea)

saffūrá, (pl.) *saffūr* beads for making a belt

safī, -he, -hīn, -hāt (comm. pl.) *safaha* foolish, silly, stupid-looking

safiná, -āt drought

safra yellow guinea corn

sāg (f.), (d.) *-ēn,* (pl.) *sīgān* leg (from the knee down)

sāg, busūg drive animals; blow (of wind)

sagadé, (coll.) *ságade* pumpkin

sagam, bisugum sew

sagat, busugut be cold

saggar, bisaggir set on fire

sagir, (pl.) *sugūr* vulture

sāgit, sāgte, -īn, -āt cold (inanim.)

sahabá, (coll.) *sahāb* cloud

sahāra ~ *sahārt alxala* desert

sahī, sahīhe, (pl.) *suhā(h)* true, truthful

sāhi, -ye, -yīn, -yāt honest, candid, truthful

sahīb ~ *sāhib, -e,* (pl.) *ashāb* friend; owner

sāhib māl (no pl.) rich (man)

sāhirinna, sāhirinha, sāhirinhīn, -āt hexed (result of the 'evil eye', usually cast by women)

sāʾa, -āt clock, watch; hour; luck
 ___ (*-tak*) *kam* What time is it?
 ___ *-tak di gursaha kam* How much does this watch cost?

saʾal, bis(ʾ)al ask a question, demand

saʾīd, -e, -īn, -āt lucky

saʾīd Said (p.n.m.)

sāʾit while, when (conj.)
 ___ *anīna fi kalāmna jā* While we were talking, he came.
 ___ *anīna nilkallam hu jā* While we were talking, he came.

sāǰal, bisāǰal hurry up

saǰan, bisǰin ~ *busǰun* imprison, jail

sāk sock(s)

sākan, bisākin drive away

sakat, buskut be quiet

sākin Sakin (p.n.m.)
___ *-e* Sakine (p.n.f.)

sākit gratis, free (of charge)

sakka, busukk kick

sakkar, bisakkir lock

sakkāri, sakkāra, -īn, -āt drunkard

sakkat, bisakkit quiet (s.o.)

sakkīn (f.), (pl.) *sakākīn* knife
___ *ambrēdīl* long knife
___ *qalīde* big knife

sakkūt (m.), (pl.) *sukkāt* quiet

sakrān, -a, -īn, -āt introvert

sāl (sg./pl.) bracelet for upper arm

sāl, bisīl flood, overflow

salab, bi/uslub undress, molt

salām peace

sālam, bisālim greet, say 'hello'

salax, busulux cut open, skin

salga latrine

sall(a), bisill(a) dismiss, fire, sack (s.o.); pursue; bring s.t. out

sallam, bisallim say 'good-bye' to s.o.
___ *(ala)* greet, say 'hello'

salṭānīye sultanate

sām, busūm fast (v.)

sama sky

sāma, bisāmi forgive

samaká, (coll.) *samak* fish

sa/eme, sa/emha, -īn -āt good, handsome, nice

samīn, -e, (pl.) *sumān* fat (adj.)

sami/ux gum (Arabic)

samm (no pl.) poison

samma, bisammi name (v.)
___, *bisumm qašim-* close one's mouth

sammam, bisammin poison (v.)

sammat, bisammit laugh at

samūm hot wind

sana, (pls.) *sinīn* ~ *sanawāt* year

sanad, bisnud pick up, raise

sanam superstition

sanda Sanda (p.n.m.)

sanda bēḍa white cloth

sandal wood used as incense for burning

sāniye, -āt deep well

sankarāy, (pl.) *sankara* robber

sanna, bisinn sharpen

sansan, bisansin sniff

sanṭal, -āt big kettle for boiling water

saqāra youth

saqayyir, saqayre, -īn, -āt small, young

saqīr, -e, (pls.) *suq/ʾār* small
___ (m./f.), *-īn, -āt,* (comm. pls.) *(ī)yāl* ~ *ōlād* child, baby, infant, toddler

sār, bisīr go, leave, journey
___ *(l-)* migrate

sara, bisra (b-) care, take care of; feed, graze, pasture, take to pasture

sāra, bisāra lend (s.t.); wrestle with one another

sarāb mirage

sarag ~ *sirig, busrug* steal, kidnap

sarax, bi/usrux rear, shout, hiss

sarfanǰi kind of tree in bush

sa/erīme (pl.) *sarāyim* bridle

sarǰ, (pl.) *surūǰ* saddle (of wood)

sarra, bisarri (b-) (take to) pasture

sarra, busurr wrap

sarraf, bisarrif li ʾamur- take care of s.o.'s needs

sarrāg, -a, -īn, -āt, (comm. pls.) *masarge* ~ *sarārīg* thief

sarrār (no pl.) cricket

sarti time, chance, opportunity; when, while (conj.)
(___*ad*)*darat* harvest time (Nov.-Dec.)
___ *anīna fi kalāmna ǰā* While we were talking, he came.
___ *anīna nilkallam hu ǰā* While we were talking, he came,
___ *wāhid* sometimes

sās marrow

sāsa gambling

sāt, bisīt almaktūb cover a book

satar, bustur bury

sāti, -ye, -sātīn, sātiyāt sixth; Saturday, weekend

saṭṭa, busuṭṭ slap

sawa same, similar, together, equal, equivalent

sawwa, bisawwi do, make, use
___ *fissināʾāt* do one's work, be occupied in one's profession
___ *gadé* repeat
___ *ʾazumá* celebrate
___ *ǰǰalāla* pray
___ *kalāwa* console
___ *širi lalmanša* He is ready to go.
___ *šōra* play a trick on s.o.
___ *yābis* dry, empty (v.)
___ *zulum* terrorize

sawwāgi, (pl.) *sawwāgīn* driver

sawwaṭ, bisawwiṭ beat, whip, spank

sawwe gadé Do it again!

saxal, (pl.) *suxulān* male kid (goat)
___ *-á, -āt* female kid (goat)

sāxin, sāxna, -īn, -āt. hot, warm

saxxān, -āt kettle

sāyid, sāyde, -īn, -āt fitting, proper, suitable

sayīda, -āt lady

sayyād, -īn hunter

sayyārá, -āt car, truck, lorry

sayyāri, sayyāra, -īn, -āt nomad

se until
___ *dahadda* quite
___ *hassa dugō* at last
___ *ʾambākir* See you later!
___ *kan* unless
___ *šiya/šie* See you later!

sēbé, (pl.) *sēbayāt* barn

sēf, (pl.) *sawafa* sword

se/ame, se/amhe, -īn, -āt nice, good, handsome

sēr, (pl.) *siyūr* hide, leather thong

serīr, (pls.) *surūr* ~ *sarāʾ/yir* bed

sēs, (pls.) *si/uyūs* cushioned chair, throne

seyūra (no pl.) journey, transport

sib(h)e, (pl.) *siba* worry beads, rosary

sīd, (pls.) *siyād(a)* owner
___ *addangá* drummer
___ *addarb* (pl.) ___ *addurūb* guide
___ *aǰǰumāl* camel driver
___ *alkabāyir* braggart
___ *alqayta* flutist
___ *assuxum* heathen (person)
___ *attaši* taxi driver
___ *qašim* (m.) obnoxious, rude, impertinent (person), 'big mouth'

sidda ddarb Close the door!

siddāda, -āt lid
___ *-t albarrād,* (pl.) *-āt albarrādāt* teapot lid
___ *-t algazzāzá* bottle cap

si/uffārá, (pls.) *safāfīr* ~ *sawāfir* long flute

sifir zero

sigēr, -āt small vulture

sihir (no pl.) magic

siǰin, (pl.) *suǰūn* prison

sikin, biskun live

silāh, (pl.) *aslihe* weapon

silay, (pl.) *sa'ālu* cannibal

sile shilling (= 10 kobo)

silik, (pl.) *silūk* telegraph, telephone line

sillāy, -e, -īn, -āt wizard

silta black snake

simenti cement floor

simī, bisma hear, understand; speak a foreign language

simin, bismun become fat

simmēné, (coll.) *simmēn* flying ant

sīn (no pl.) small water skin

si/unā'a, -āt job, trade, profession

sinīnak kam How old are you?

sinkīte, (pl.) *sanākīt* hump

sinn, (pl.) *sunūn* tooth
 ___ *alfīl* ivory (lit., 'elephant tooth')

sinyāka white fine sand

sirēsir, (pl.) *sirsirāt* narrow path(way)

sirge stealing

sirr, (pl.) *asrār* secret

sirriyé, -āt concubine

sirsir, (pl.) *sarāsir* chain

sirwāl ~ *sruwāl,* (pl.) *sarāwīl* pants, trousers

sitte six

sittīn sixty

siwām fasting

siyād attarbiye educated people who do not follow the Koran

siyāsi, siyāsīya, siyāsīyīn, -āt political

sō'ar, bisō'ar be mad (of dogs only)

so'ol ~ *suq/ɣ(u)l* ~ *su'ul* (no pls.) something, thing

sōǰa army

sōm (religious) fast

sōrá, (pl.) *sawāro* room

sōsal, -āt large grass basket

sōsal Sosal (p.n.m.)

sōsō sock(s)

sōṭ, (pl.) *sīṭān* whip

sper, -īn driver

sūb ley 'alme Pour me some water!

subhānaḷḷāhi By God!/Good heavens!

subū morning, 6:00 A.M. to 8:00 A.M.

sūfá, (coll.) *sūf* hair, body hair, animal hair, wool, feather
 ___ *-t anna'ām* ostrich feather

sufra, (pl.) *sifar* big tin plate

sūg, (pl.) *sawaga* market (place)

su'āl, -āt question

su'ul (no pl.) problem

sukkur sugar
 ___ *dagīg/gāri* granulated sugar
 ___ *darādim hana lbikēt* sugar cube

sulb, (pl.) *sulūb* waist

sulhu arbitration, reconciliation

sulṭān, (pl.) *salāṭīn* sultan, head of village, king

summ name

summ qaši/amak Close your mouth!/Shut up!

sumsum sesame, couscous

suq/ɣ(u)l ~ *su'ul* ~ *so'ol* (no pls.) thing, something

sūra, -āt picture

sūrá, -āt chapter of Koran

surra, (pl.) *surar* navel, belly button

sūsá, (coll.) *sūs* bug, worm

suwār (sg./pl.) bracelet

suwēg, -āt little market

suxum heathenism

swētir, (pl.) *swētāt* sweater

Ṣ

ṣabar, buṣ(u)bur endure, be patient

ṣabī, (pls.) *ṣi/ubyān* young man, boy

ṣābir, -a, -īn, -āt patient (adj.)

ṣabur patience

ṣabūr, -a, -īn, -āt very patient

ṣadir, (pl.) *ṣudūr* breast, chest, bosom

ṣaff, (pl.) *ṣuffi* side (anat.)

ṣaffar, biṣaffar become yellow

ṣalā prayer
  ṣalāt adduhur afternoon prayer
  ___ *al'īšá* nighttime prayer
  ___ *al'uṣúr* evening prayer
  ___ *almuq/ɣri/ub* sunset prayer
  ___ *assubū/alfaǰir* morning prayer

ṣalla, biṣalli pray

ṣandūx, (pl.) *ṣanādīx* box

ṣaṇṇāṭ, -a, -īn, -āt listener

ṣāt, buṣūt cook or prepare food

ṣawwāt, -e, -īn, -āt cook

ṣēde, (coll.) *ṣēd* antelope; game, prey

ṣēf summer

Š

šaba as, like, similar to
  ___ *da* (*ke*) same thing, like this, for example

šābu, bišabi resemble

šaba(*h*) same thing
  ___ *tawā'* usually
  ___ *tawā'* (*ke*) *bas nimši* We usually go.

(*šabā*[*h*]) *lešinu* why?

šabaká, -āt bag

šabah ṭaw(*w*)*a* as (like) before

šabaš/k spider web

šabat, bi/ušbut follow and overtake, meet

šab'ān, -a, -īn, -āt satiated, content, satisfied

šadará, (coll.) *šadar* tree

šadda strength, violence

šadda, bišidd load or saddle an animal

šadīd, -e, -īn, -āt, (comm. pl.) *šudād* violent

šadūdú, (pl.) *šadayıd* camel or horse blanket

šāf, bišīf see
  ___ *fi darb-* expect
  ___ *fōg* look through
  ___ *fōg annafīza* He looked through the window.
  ___ *-ak gabul inta ma tič* He saw you before you came.

šagga, bišu/igg split (intr.)
  ___ *baṭina* cut one's stomach (ceremonially)
  ___ *dātēn* be early
  ___ *filhūt* catch fish

šaggag, bišaggig split (tr.)

šagīge (no pl.) headache

šagiyān, -a, -īn, -āt ungrateful

šaglab, bišaglib turn upside down

šahad, biš(h)ad beg

šahag, bišag hiccough

šahar, (d.) *-ēn,* (pls.) *tuš(h)ur* ~ *šuhūr* month

šaharīye salary, wages

šahhād, -īn beggar

šāhid, (pl.) *šuhūd* witness

ša'ar hair (on woman's head)
____ *-i* my hair (for women)

ša'āwa concern, interest; pleasure

ša'īr barley

šāk, bušūk do s.t. bad (a bad act)

šaka, biški complain

šakar, biškur thank

šākir, -e, -īn, -āt grateful

šakk (no pl.) doubt

šakkak, bišakkik doubt (v.)

šākūš handbag

šakwa, -āt complaint

šāl, -e, -īn, -āt fair (of weather)

šāl, bišīl carry, take
____ *aṣṣabur* have patience
____ *dēn* borrow
____ *wa'ad* contract (with s.o.)

šāle (m./f.) (very) kind, good to everyone

šalxá, (pl.) *šilōx* cut

šam (f.) sun

šamāta malicious glee

šam'āyá ~ *šahamá,* (coll.) *šaham* animal fat, grease (for cooking)

šamm, bišimm smell (tr.)

šammām (no pl.) tide

šān because, due to

šanab, -āt moustache

šānge, (pl.) *šāngiyāt* mosquito net

šaqalān, -a, -īn, -āt busy

šaqqal, bišaqqil interrupt

šār, bišīr give s.o. money to buy s.t. for oneself; refuse to return borrowed money

šara, bišri sell, buy

šarāb (no pl.) drink

šarad, bišrud escape

šarak, (pl.) *šurukke* net
____ *alfār,* (pl.) ____ *lfār* mouse or rat trap

šaram, bišrum wound (v.)

šarārá, (coll.) *šarār* spark

šaraṭ, bušruṭ tear, rip (tr.)

šāri, (pls.) *šīrān* ~ *šawāri* path(way), street

šārib, (pl.) *šawārib* moustache

šārid, -e, -īn, -āt deserter

šarīf, -īye, šarīfīn, -āt person who touches fire without getting burned

šarī'e courthouse

šarīk (no pl.) business partner

šarīye, (pl.) *mašara* judge

šarmūṭá, (pl.) *šarāmīṭ* prostitute

šarmūṭá, (coll.) *šarmūṭ* dried meat, jerky

šarr money given to help others

šarr, -e, -īn, -āt evil (adj./n.), danger, blame

šarra, bušurr put outside to dry

šarraṭ, bišarrit tear, rip (tr.)

šarṭ, (pl.) *šurūṭ* circumstance, condition

šatta, bišitt go somewhere

š/ǰattat, bišattit scatter, spread, throw around or away; collapse

šāṭir, -a, (pls.) *-īn* ~ *šiṭār, -āt* clever, smart

šawa, bišwi roast

šāwaf, bišāwif (min) see each other

šāwar, bišāwir consult, discuss

šāwara/e advice

šawwaf, bišawwif look or see into the future

šawwāfa, -āt mirror

šawwāf(i), -a, -īn, -āt seer, magician, sorcerer

šaxar, busxur roar, shout

šaxi, -ye, šaxīn, -āt generous, kind

šaxxar, bišaxxir snore

šāyib, (pl.) *šiyāb* old man

šayyab, bišayyib be(come) old, grow old, age (of men)

šayyāl, -a/e, -īn, -āt carrier, porter

šayyāla, -āt knapsack; truck, lorry

še (no pl.) thing, something

šēbe ground seeds used for women's hair grooming or body decoration

šēda, -āt certificate, passport

šēdá witness

šeʾīni, šeʾīni, šeʾūni, šeʾinni Take me!/Come with me!/Escort me!

šēl (no pl.) load

šellūfa, (pl.) *šalālīf* lip

šēn, -e, -īn, -āt wretched

šeršer, bišeršer buy

šēt sock(s)

šēx, (pl.) *šiyūx* ruler, chief, amir

šibī, bišbah be satisfied

šidēre, -āt small tree

šidik, (pls.) *ši/udūk* cheek

šie little, small (thing), few

šifta fi bukān hājira I saw him in another place.

šifta sinīn tinēn ʾagaban ~ šifta fi santēn I saw him two years ago.

šiʾir ~ šaʾar hair (on woman's head)

šikk another, more, different, special

šinib, (pl.) *šunūb* lip ring

šinu what (interr./rel.)
 ___ *lbukūn bibga murr bilēn* What will happen will be very sad.
 ___ *lkān/alligīk* What's the matter?
 ___ *lkān almurr ke* What happened was very sad.
 ___ *lkāyin* What's happening?

širgānīye, (pls.) *šarāgīn ~ -āt* kind of grass used for mats and ceilings; adobe block used for fences or ceilings

širib, bišrab drink
 ___ *alwahāla* be inconvenienced
 ___ *attāba* smoke (a cigarette)
 ___ *rī(h)* exercise

širka, -āt company

šite winter; harmattan

šitta (sg./pl.) (chili) pepper
 ___ *dugāg* chilies

šī/ēṭān(e), (pl.) *šawāṭīn* devil, Satan

šiya ~ šie ~ šwīya little, small (thing), few
 ___ *ke* a little later, later on
 ___ *šiya* slightly, slowly, little by little

šōf seeing (v.n.), appearance, sight
 ___ *-a fasil* squinty-eyed

šōká, (pl.) *šōk* thorn (tree)

šok/ʾolat annār flame

šorá, -āt proposal, advice; trick

šugg half

šuggá, (pl.) *šugūg* small grass mat

šukur gratitude, thanks; Thanks!

šūm act, good deed, modesty

šūna (no pl.) load

šuwāl, -āt sack

šwīya little, small (thing), few

T

tāb, butūb regret, repent, ask for forgiveness

taba, bitba follow

tāba, -āt tobacco, cigarette
 ___ *malwīye* pipe (for smoking)

tabasá, (pl.) *tabas* tuft of hair

tabbas, bitabbis plow

tabbat, bitabbit be certain or sure

tābi, -ye, tābīn, -āt follower

tafkīr thinking

tafsīr explanation, commentary or exegesis of the Koran

tagdīm (no pl.) offer

taggal, bitaggil make heavy

tagīl, -e, (pl.) *tugāl* heavy

taham, bitham suspect

t/dahar, bit(h)ar ~ bittar prevent

taharīš provocation

tahit below, under

taʾab occupation

taʾabān, -a, -īn, -āt tired

t(aʾ)āl Come!
 ___ *āxar* Come later!
 ___ *bilmāla* Come slowly/carefully!
 ___ *dātēn* Come early!
 ___ *dāxil* Come inside!
 ___ *fi waqt alwaʾad* Come on time!
 ___ *gadé* Come again!
 ___ *ǰāy* Come here!
 ___ *ladafti* Come to my side!

taʾallam, bitʾallam learn

taʾazīye/a, -āt condolence, sympathy

taʾʾab, bitiʾʾib make s.o. tired

tāǰar, bitāǰir trade

tāǰir, (pls.) *tuǰǰār(a) ~ tuǰǰārīn* trader, merchant

takam, bitakim prevent

tákarče (assortment of) things, odds and ends

takīya, -āt side (wall) of a house (inside or outside)

takke all

talāta three
 ___ *ʾalif* three thousand

talātīn thirty

talfān, -a, -īn, -āt foolish, stupid; spoiled by parents; unusable

tālīm education

tālit, tālte, -īn, -āt third (ordinal)

talǰ kind of sugar

tallaf, bitallif spoil, damage, ruin
 ___ *māl (fin subbāt)* spend money (on s.o.)

talūl, -a, -īn, -āt slow(-moving/-learning)

tamad (sg./pl.) shallow well

tamaliye cotton seed

tamām exactly, at last; splendid, fantastic; polite

taman cost, price
 ___ *-a kam* How much is it?; How much does it cost?

tāman, bitāmin bargain

tamāni eight

tamānīn eighty

tambal, -āt small hand drum

tambūna white guinea corn

tamīme, (pl.) *tamāyim* amulet

tāmin, -e, -īn, -āt eighth (ordinal)

tami/urá, (colls.) *tami/ur* date (palm)

tamma, butumm finish (tr.)

tammam, bitammim finish (tr.)

tammat 'The End' (what a storyteller says when the story is over)

tamtam, bitamtim stammer, stutter

tana, bitina fold paper

tanaká, (coll.) *tanak* tin, tin can

tandal, (pl.) *tanādil* heap of dirt

tandu (sg./pl.) small leather bag for oil

tāni, -ye, tānīn, tāniyāt second (ordinal); a second time, again

taqamqam, bitaqamqim grumble

tār revenge (n.)

tara (negative tag-question marker)

tara, bitar stop (tr.)

tarak, butruk abandon

tarāni ma banši He stopped me from going.

tarba, bitarbi teach, educate

tarbiye education, culture

tārīx history

tarǰam, bitarǰim translate

tarǰumān, -a, -īn, -āt translator

tarr, bitirr alxēṭ spin cotton

tarra, bitirr clean up

tartab, bitartab arrange, make an arrangement with, find help for

tartīb arrangement

tāsi, -ye, tāsīn, tāsiyāt ninth

taši taxi

tašša, bitišš ignite, burn (tr.)

taššāsá, -āt skewer

tawa (very) same
 ___ *kulla* before all this

tawarāya ~ *tawará,* (coll.) *tōr,* (pls.) *tīrān* ~ *tawār* bull, ox

taw(w)a used to (v.)
 ___ *bihaǰǰir* He used to beg.
 ___ *nugud fi kāno* I used to live in Kano.

tawwamat, titawwim give birth to twins

tayte (no pl.) boat made of grass (usually on Lake Chad)

tēbir, (pl.) *tēbrāt* table

tēbur, -āt shovel

tēma, -āt strainer (usually for tea)

tērab seeds
 ___, *bitērib* sow

tēs, (pl.) *tuyūs* billy goat

tētalá, (coll.) *tētil,* (pl.) *tayātil* deer

tibin (sg./pl.) grass used for roofs; blanket for donkey's back

tič fillēl la/ankūn ma tič Either you come tonight or you don't.

tigarri teaching

tigdar tigra You are able to read.

ti'ib, bitab be(come) tired
 ___ *malāy* He is more tired than I.

ti'illim teaching

tiǰāra commerce, trade, business

tikaffi kam How much does it cost?

tīlas must

tilif, bitilaf spoil (intr.)

tilīle playing and conversation activity at night

timsā(h), (pls.) *tamāsī(h)* crocodile

tinēn(i) ~ *it(i)nēn* two
 ___ *haw šišiye* two and six (2½ shillings = 25 kobo)

t(i)rāb dirt, ground; dirty

tirbin, (pl.) *tarābin* small fish net

t(i)rīle, (pls.) *tarāhīl* ~ *tarāyil* marriage ceremony

tirimbal (no pl.) kind of small drum

tirmiye bēḍa white cloth

tis'e nine

tis'īn ninety

tīt(āni) below, under; lower (adj.)

tōb measure of length (6, 8, or 10 yds.)

tōb, (pl.) *tībān* gown

tōba repentance

tōč flashlight

tom kind of tree in bush

tōm, -a, -tīmān, tōmāt twin

tugul weight

tuhuma, -āt suspicion

tuǰǰāra business

tūkotūko by or with force, forcefully

tulut (one-)third

tūmá, (coll.) *tūm* garlic

tumfār different

tumtum kind of song and dance game played by females

tur + impf. Don't . . . ! (for family members)

turbo cow path

turud dugō timši lebakāna Then she turned back and went to his place.

tūta (sg./pl.) flag

Ṭ

ṭabag, (pl.) *ṭubāg* hoof, sole of animal's foot; big grass plate
 ___ *hana ǰǰumāl* camel hoof
 ___ *hana lfīl* elephant hoof

ṭabag, buṭubug bend, fold (in two)

ṭabaz, buṭubuz pierce

ṭabbal, biṭabbil lock

ṭabīʾa/e character, disposition, nature; tradition

ṭābi/ul, -āt table

ṭābūrá, (pl.) *ṭābūr* parade

ṭafalá ~ *ṭufulān, -a,* (pls.) *ṭi/uful* baby, infant, toddler

ṭaffal, biṭaffil become mad, crazy or senile

ṭāgé ~ *ṭāgīye, -āt* hat, cap

ṭagga, buṭugg knock, tap
 ___ *(li) ʾīda* clap

ṭaggāg pulse

ṭāgīti my hat/cap

ṭāgīye, -āt hat, cap
 ___ *-t naṣ̤āra* helmet

ṭahhar, biṭahhir clean, purify; circumcise

ṭāhir, -e, -īn, -āt clean, pure

ṭahūr circumcision

ṭāʾa obedience
 ___, *biṭāʾa* obey

ṭaʾām (seasoned) food, nourishment, taste

ṭaʾan ~ *ṭāna, biṭan* slash or wound (with a knife), gore
 ___, (pl.) *ṭuʾūn* slash
 ___, *biṭʾan* give

ṭāʾim, -e, -īn, -āt tasty, (too) sweet

ṭāʾūn, (pl.) *ṭawāʾīn* cut from a knife, spear or arrow, incision; hernia

ṭak(u)wa There is . . . over there; There he/it is.

ṭāl, buṭūl become tall

ṭala, biṭla rise

____ *barra* go outside
____ (*fōg*) climb

ṭalab, buṭulub (*min*) ask for, request

ṭalag, buṭulug divorce (v.)

ṭalāg divorce (n.)

ṭalas, buṭ(u)lus set (tr.); smear, smooth a surface with cement, plaster
____ (*albēt*) *basimenti* plaster (a house) with cement

ṭālib, -a, (pl.) *ṭullāb* student

ṭalha kind of tree in bush

ṭalīge (no pl.) fire set in bush for agricultural purposes

ṭalla, biṭalli (help) climb

ṭallag, biṭallig free; divorce

ṭallāy ladder

ṭalū rising (of sun)

ṭama greed, stinginess
____, *biṭma* (*fi*) long or yearn (for)

ṭamalá, (pls.) *ṭamal*(*āt*) big water hole, reservoir

ṭamalēge kind of green vegetable (available only during rainy season)

ṭamas, buṭumus sink, disappear

ṭamātir (sg./pl.) tomato

ṭamʾān, -a, -īn, -āt profitable

ṭammal, biṭammil become muddy (of water)

ṭammas, buṭumus drown

ṭammāy, -a, -īn, -āt greedy

ṭān, biṭan ʾibri/e vaccinate

ṭāna ~ *ṭaʾan, biṭan* wound or slash (with a knife), gore

ṭāná, (pl.) *ṭuʾunne* wound

ṭār, buṭūr fly

ṭarad, buṭ(u)rud chase, pursue; send away, fire (s.o.)

ṭaraf, (pl.) *ṭurūf* side (location)
____ *albahar* (river) shore
____ *alhaǰar* cliff
____ *alhille* section of town

ṭaragá, (pl.) *ṭarag* word
____ *ṭaragá* word by word

ṭaraš, buṭruš knock down

ṭarbūš red hat or cap, tarboosh

ṭarīd, (pl.) *ṭurdān* younger brother
____ *-e,* (pl.) *-āt* younger sister

ṭarīg, -āt chance

ṭarī(h), ṭarīhe, -īn , -āt clean, pure, fresh

ṭarīn, -e, (pl.) *ṭurun* sharp, thin-edged

ṭarra, biṭirr move
____, *buṭurr* line up

ṭarrak, biṭarrik sharpen

ṭaršān, -a, -īn, -āt deaf

ṭāsá, (coll.) *ṭās* bowl, dish, tin plate

ṭašša, buṭušš put food on a cooking grate

ṭaššās, -a, -īn, -āt ugly

ṭawa, biṭwi roll up (tr.)

ṭawīl, -e ~ *ṭi/ayīle,* (pls.) *ṭu/iwāl* long, tall, deep

ṭaw(*w*)*a* before, formerly, previously

ṭawwal too long (of time)
_, *biṭawwil* spend or waste time (doing s.t.)
____ *ley* He wasted my time.

ṭaxīn, -e, -īn, -āt hard to break

ṭay, -e, -īn, -āt kind

ṭayʾan, biṭayʾin cut with a knife, spear or arrow

ṭāyir, ṭāyre, -īn, -āt flying

ṭayyab, biṭayyib make s.o. happy

ṭayyāra, -āt airplane

ṭayyib, ṭayybe, ṭayy(i)bīn, -āt all right, well, fine [response to greeting; *-īn* form most common]

ṭērá, (coll.) *ṭēr,* (pl.) *ṭuyūr* bird

ṭēre evil eye

ṭīb seeds for women's hair grooming

ṭihhāra circumcision

ṭimi, biṭma gain, make a profit

ṭīne, (coll.) *ṭīn* clay, mud

ṭorōro kind of tree or grass used for making small reed rafts

ṭūbá, (coll.) *ṭūb* adobe

ṭūl distance, height; entirety
 ___ *-a* for/in a long time

ṭumā greed, stinginess

ṭuwāli straight (adv.)

U

u and

ubdīye slavery

ūd, (pl.) *īdān* piece of wood; walking stick, cane
 ____ *alharbá* wood for making a spear
 ____ *almasīč* minaret

ugayá, -āt head pad to cushion a load

ugda, (pl.) *ugād* knot

ugub after
 ____ *(hu)da* after this, afterwards

uǰra rent (n.)

ūm, -i, -u, -an Swim!

umrak kam How old are you?

umur life, age

urd width

urūdu kind of animal

úsub(i), (pls.) *asābe/i* finger

usubí my finger

usum ~ *isim* ~ *summ,* (pl.) *asmā* name

usura immediately

usuṭ middle, midst (of), center

uṣúr late afternoon (4:00 P.M. to 6:00 P.M.)

u/iwārá, (pl.) *awāwīr* sore, wound

W

wa (interr. particle [inanim. subj.])
indak filus ___ Do you have money?

wačal(āy)á, (pl.) *wačāli* pole for holding up a house

wadā, buwudd māla deposit money

wadda, b(u)waddi move; take

wadda, (f.) *waddaytīye* dwarf

waddab, biʾ/waddib train (animals)

waddar, biwaddir (*l-*) lose, waste (money/time)

wadī cowry

wādi countryside

wādīn, -āt some, several

wāḍi, -he, -hīn, -hāt clear, pure

wafka ~ *wakfa* pause, wait (n.)

wagā, biga fall (down), set (of sun)

wāga kind of bird

wagaf ~ *wigif* ~ *wifig, bigīf* stop (intr.)

waggaf, biwaggif stop (tr.)

waggar, biwaggir work for

wāgi, -ye, wāgīn, -āt falling down

wāgif, wāfge, -īn, -āt upright

wahad, būhad swear, take an oath

wahad ~ *wehed* + pron. suff. alone

wāhade wāhade in detail

wahāla inconvenience

wahāt By the life of . . . ! [oath formula]
___ *abuy* By the life of my father!
___ *dīni* By the life of my religion!

wahīd, -e, -īn, -āt (*min*) different (from)

wāhed, (f.) *wāhade* one

waʾadá, (pl.) *waʾad* promise, contract

waʾalēkum min assalām Greetings! [response to traditional Muslim greeting]

waʾara ~ *wāra,* (pl.) *waʾarāt* forest

waʾazi warning

wajā, biwāj(h)i cause pain
___, (pl.) *-ʾāt* illness, disease
___ *bilēn* serious illness
___ *lmafāsil* rheumatism

wajaǰ (no pl.) rope made from animal skin

wajāni wajāk (formula for introducing a story or riddle) [lit., 'And it came to me, and it is coming to you . . . ']

wājib appropriate, proper, right, true; necessary, incumbent upon

wakāla restlessness

wakīl, -e, -īn, -āt restless (person); assistant

wakkad, biwakkid assure

wakkal, biwakkil appoint

wakkat, biwakkit make certain or sure

w/balā without [See phrases under *b/wala*]

wāla, biwāli hit (animals) with a stone or arrow

wal(ad) ~ *wald,* (pls.) *ōlād* ~ *(ī)yāl* boy; servant
wal halāl law-abiding Muslim
___ *ʾimm,* (pl.) *(ī)yāl ʾimm* (male, paternal) cousin
___ *nās* person of well-to-do family (m.sg.)
___ *walad* grandson
___ *xāl,* (pl.) *(ī)yāl xāl* (male, maternal) cousin
___ *ziná* bastard
walad, (pl.) *(ī)yāl (aššadara)* fruit
wald, (pl.) *(ī)yāl ajjimmēz* fig
___ *alharām* bastard
___ *alʾaxu(t)* nephew

___ *alkalb/alhumār/alʾaqalaf/albūmi* (kinds of curses)
___ *almulk* person of good class/grade (m.)

wālaf, biwālif be accustomed or used to

wālid, -īn father
___ *-e, -āt* mother
___ *-ē/īn* parents

walla or

wallāda, -āt midwife

wālo eggplant

walūda, -āt birth

wal̤l̤a (interr. particle [anim. subj.])
inta ʾāfi ___ Are you well?

wan nukā [assim. from *wal nukā*] law-abiding Muslim

wāqaf, biwāqif be fortunate

waqár sweat (n.)

waqa/it time

waqīla maybe, perhaps

waqqar, biwaqqir sweat

waqqārá, -āt undergarment, undershirt, lining of man's long gown

waqrān, -a, -īn, -āt sweating, perspiring

wa/era ~ *wēra, biwe/ari* ~ *bēri* show

warā̕ behind, in back of, after
___ *(l)bēt,* (pls.) ___ *lb(i/u)yūt* toilet

warad, buʾurud ~ *būrud (l-)* fetch, lead an animal (to water), want to bring (water)

waradde predawn

waragá, (coll.) *warag* leaf; paper; leather amulet worn around the neck, containing excerpts from Koran

waraké ~ *wir(i)k* (f.), (ds.) *-ēn,* (pls.) *wurūk* ~ *wurukke* thigh

waralá, (coll.) *waral,* (pl.) *wárala* iguana

warāni straight backwards

wardān, -a ~ *wirde, -īn, -āt* not well, ill (with fever)

wārim, wārme, -īn, -āt swollen

warrāni last; upper

warwar, biwarwir spin (s.o.) around
___, *biwarwur* cause pain

wasax dirt, filth

wasī, -ʾe, (pls.) *wusā* ~ *wasīʾīn, wusā* ~ *wasīʾāt* wide

wassax, biwassix make dirty

wassāy alagōgo watch maker or repairman

waswas, biwaswis (fi galba) talk to oneself

waswās conscience

wasxān, -a, -īn, -āt dirty

wāṣ̤a, biwāṣ̤i (l-) repair, fix, clean; prepare (a place), make ready

waṣafa, -āt description

wāṣ̤al, b(i)wāṣ̤al arrive

waṣ̤alān arrival

waṣīye (no pl.) will, testament

waṣṣa, biwaṣṣi advise, recommend

waṣṣaf, biwaṣṣif describe

waṣ̤ṣ̤al, biwaṣ̤ṣ̤il arrive, reach

watīr/le, (colls.) *watīr/l,* (pl.) *watāyir* car, truck, lorry, bus, vehicle

waṭā̕ air, sky, atmosphere, climate, weather (m. or f.); ground, dirt, area (f.)

waxt chance, opportunity

wayhe Alas!/Woe!

wa/uzarā council of chiefs or rulers

wazīr(i), (pls.) *wa/uzarā* chief, (government) minister, vizier

wehed ~ *wahad* + pron. suff. alone

wē(ʾ) yes

wēʾa, biwāʾi wake (s.o.) up

wēke gravy, sauce, soup

wēla north

wēn where?

w/yēnu, -i, -um, -an which (one)?

wēy + nominal sentence pretend to

___ *hu marḍān* He pretended to be sick.

wigif ~ *wifig* ~ *wagaf, bigīf* stop (intr.)

wihim, būham guess, think, feel

wiǰih ~ *wiǰhi* ~ *wu/ičih,* (pls.) *wač/ǰaha* ~ *wuǰū* face

wildat, tuwulud ~ *tilítt* ~ *tilda* give birth, bring forth

wilēd, -īn son, little boy

wilid, buwulud give birth, bring forth

wirid, būrud be unwell

wir(i)k lap [See also *waraké*]

wisix, būsix become dirty

wiṣil, biṣal ~ *būṣil* ~ *bwaṣel* arrive, reach

witid peg, stake

wīya with

wizza/e, -āt goose

(w)ōgad, biw/ʾōgid light a fire

wudā deposit (n.)

wuḍū ablution

wulēd, -īn baby, infant, toddler (m.)

wurdān, (pl.) *warādīn* throat, windpipe, trachea

wurum, buwaram swell up, become swollen

wusādá, (pls.) *-āt* ~ *wasāyid* cushion, pillow
___ *-t ʾassis* cushioned chair

wusé, wusēki, -ku, -kan Bravo!/Well done!/ Welcome back!

wu/azarā council of chiefs or rulers [pl. of *wazīr(i)*]

X

xabar, (pls.) *(a)xubār* story, tale, news
___/*(a)xubār fi* Is there any news?
___ *attawa* history
___ *azzamān* current news
___ *naḍīf* good news

xabar + pron. suff. why?/what for?
___*-a bibki* What's wrong with him? He's crying.

xabaš ~ *xašab* kind of tree in bush

xabaṭ, buxubuṭ ~ *baxabiṭ* hurt, beat, hit, give s.o. a blow, flog

xabbar, bixabbir tell, relate, mention, inform

xabbaṭ, bixabbiṭ hit, beat

xābīr, -e, -īn, -āt bearer of news; guide

xabīs, -e, -īn, -āt dirty, wicked (person), rascal

xabṭa, -āt blow, hit (n.)

xadam, baxadam do, accomplish
___ *(l-)* serve

xadāma livestock tax

xadāmt albagar cattle tax

xadd, (pl.) *xudūd* cheek

xadda, buxudd mix, stir; cook, prepare gruel

xaddam bixaddim hire

xaddām, -a, -īn, -āt worker (m.), steward
___ *alfarāw* leather worker
___ *anniʾille* shoemaker
___ *-a, -āt* worker (f.), stewardess
___ *-a fi llubtān* nurse

xādum (m./f.), (comm. pls) *xawādim* ~ *a/ebīd* servant

xaḍará, (coll.) *xaḍar* vegetable

xaḍḍar, bixaḍḍir dye blue or green (v.)

xāf, bixāf (min) be afraid, fear

xaffa, buxuff be(come) light (in weight)

xaffaf, bixaffif lighten (a burden)
___ *aǰǰubā* reduce tax

xāfi, -ye, xāfīn, xāfiyāt dangerous (person), madman

xafīf, -e, (pl.) *xufāf* light (weight)

xaǰilān, xaǰalāna, xaǰalānīn, -āt ashamed, shy, bashful

xaǰǰal, bixaǰǰil embarrass

xāl, (pls.) *(a)xawāl* maternal uncle
___ *-a, -āt* maternal aunt

xala bush, rural countryside, desert

xāla Khala (p.n.f.)

xālaf, bixālif go against, oppose, disobey

xalag, (pl.) *xulgān* gown

xalaq, bux(u)luq create

xalas almost
___ *tammám alʾakil* I have almost finished eating.

xalas ~ *xilis, buxulus* be complete(d), finished or all gone

xalas ~ *xālis, xālse, -īn, -āt* finished, complete(d), all gone; already
akalna xalās We have eaten already.

xalbaṭ, bixalbiṭ mix (up), confuse (s.o.)

xalbāṭi, xalbāṭīye, xalbāṭīn, -āt rascal

xāli, -ye, xālīn, -yāt empty

xalla, bixalli leave, let, give up (a habit)
___ *yamši* Let him go!
___ *yamūt* Let him die!

xallas, bixallis save (s.t.)

xallīni niǰi Let me come!

xāmis, xāmse, xāmisīn, -āt fifth (ordinal)

xamma, buxumm remove, take away

xamsa five
 ___ *ʾalf* five thousand

xamsīn fifty

xanag, bixanag choke, strangle

xanago, buxangu eclipse (intr.)

xanzīr (no pl.) pig, pork

xara, bixeri frighten, terrify

xarāb, -āt destruction, damage; old building, ruin

xaraf, bixaraf (*ʾalme*) scoop (water)

xaram, baxaram depart, leave, come out, go up, be extinguished

xaraṭ, bixaraṭ cut, scrape, carve

xarazá, (pls.) *xuruzze* ~ *xaraz* Adam's apple; beads for rosary or necklace; necklace

xarbān, -a, -īn, -āt lacking, empty; damaged, destroyed, deserted

xarīf, -āt cold season

xarīye, (pl.) *-āt* alarm, fear

xark penis
 ___ *ʾabūk*/ *ʾummak* Curse you!

xarmat, (pl.) *xarrumāt adduxān* chimney

xarra, bixarri frighten, terrify
 ___, *buxurr* leak, spill over, trickle

xarrab, bixarrib destroy

xarraf, bixarrif be cold

xarram, bixarrim bring s.t. out, escort, expel

xar(r)ūf, (pl.) *xirāf* lamb

xarrūmá, (coll.) *xarrūm* bush

xarṭūm alfīl, (pl.) *xarāṭīm alfayala* elephant trunk

xarúm kind of tree

xasa, bixasa castrate

xāsam, bixāsim quarrel with s.o., rival for a girl in marriage

xasāra, -āt loss

xāsi castrated

xasīm, -e, -īn, -āt enemy, (pl.) rivals for a girl in marriage

xasir, baxasar māla lose money

xassar, bixassir inform (tell) on s.o., report to the police; waste money, steal

xašab kind of tree in bush; wood

xatal, baxatal ~ *buxutul* escape, run away, hide

xāti/um, (pls.) *xawātim* ~ *xitam* ~ *xutumme* ring
 ___ *ala ḍān* earring

xattam, bixattim finish reading (the Koran)

xaṭa, baxaṭa mistake, make a mistake, miss a target

x/haṭab wood

xaṭaf, ba/ixaṭaf snatch, kidnap

xaṭar, bixaṭar (*l-*) journey, travel

xāṭi, -ye, xāṭīn, -yāt empty; guilty, wicked (person), troublemaker

xāṭir ~ *xaṭirān* ~ *xaṭṭāri, xaṭṭāra, -īn, -āt* traveler

x/haṭṭa, bux/huṭṭ build, put up; write a Koran tablet
 ___ *aššarr* (*fōg*) blame
 ___ *bāl* pay attention, notice
 ___ *ḍān* cup one's ear
 ___ *hankali* pay attention, notice
 ___ *ʾagil* pay attention, notice
 ___ *māl* save money

xaṭṭab, bixaṭṭib give a sermon, speech or address

xaṭṭābi, (pl.) *xaṭṭābīn* wood cutter or peddler

xaṭṭāf, -a, -īn, -āt thief who snatches s.t. and runs away, pickpocket

xaṭṭam, bixaṭṭim overtake, take a shortcut

xaṭṭāt, -a, -īn, -āt seer, sorcerer

xaṭṭēt ḍāni lakalāma I cupped my ear (with my hand) to hear him.

xawwaf, bixawwif frighten (tr.), bully

xayāl, -īn scarecrow

xayāṭa, -āt sewing needle

xayyaṭ, bixayyiṭ sew

xayyāṭ(i), -a, -īn, -āt tailor

xēma, -āt tent

xēr (no pl.) goodness

xēṭ thread

xibir, bixabar know

xidim, baxadam work (v.)

xidime labor, work (n.)

xidir, bixadar become tired

xiǰil, baxaǰal be ashamed, shy or bashful

xiǰile, (pl.) *xiǰil* humiliation, shame, shyness
 ____ *lēk/fōgak* Shame on you!

xilāf going against (n.)

xilis ~ *xalas, buxulus* be complete(d), finished or all gone

xirge, (pls.) *xarāg* ~ *xurugge* long piece of cloth wrapped around women as a dress, woman's loincloth

xirib, baxarib be destroyed

xiṭā'a fraud

xōf fear (n.)

xoff, (pl.) *axfāf* hoof

xubza type of food

xuf I was afraid.

xullu minnuku 'imši Let go (pl.)!

xumām goods, property; baggage
 ____ *albēt* furniture
 ____ *al'akil* utensils

xumša, -āt handful
 ____ *-t karas* bunch of carrots

xumus (one-)fifth

xumfur, (pl.) *xanāfir* claw (zool.); (finger)nail; kind of perfume
 ____ *arriǰil* toenail

xurs, (pl.) *xurūs* earring

xurso Khurso (p.n.m)

xurūǰ necklace

xuruz type of necklace (usually golden)

xusāra trouble

xuššā, (pl.) *xušūš* (animal) den

xušxušā, (coll.) *xušxuš* kindling wood

xuṭba, (pl.) *xuṭab* speech, address, sermon

xuṭṭ bālak/hankalak/'aglak Pay attention!/ Be careful!

xuṭṭa 'indak zēn Take care of it well!

Y

ya until

yā̕ towards; Oh!
(___) *fi/ulān, -a* so-and-so, what's-his/her-name
___ *giddām* forward
___ *mawlāy/rabbi* Oh God!
___ *warā* backwards
___ *warāši* (*ke*) afterwards

yā̕ + impf. Don't . . . ! [strong negation]
___ *tābi* Don't refuse!/Don't say no!
___ *tākul* don't eat!
___ *teddāma* It doesn't matter.
___ *tigīf* Don't stop!
___ *tiʾaxxar* Don't come late!
___ *tisawwi hu da ḍunūb* Don't do it! It's a sin.
___ *tišrab* Don't drink!
___ *tixalbinni* Don't confuse me!
___ *tudufinni* Don't bury me!
___ *tulummi* Don't blame me!

yabbas, biʾabbis dry (tr.); empty

yābis, yabsi, -īn, -āt dry (nothing inside), empty (adj.)

yādi yard (measure)

yāl ~ *īyāl* family, children [pl. of *wal*(*ad*) 'boy']

yālō (no pl.) kind of green fruit

yaḷḷa + [usually 'let's']
___ *nijri* Let's run!
___ *nimši* Let's go!
___ *nugōdu nākulu* Let's begin to eat!
___ *yaḷḷa* Hurry up!
___ *yaḷḷa* (*dugo*) *ʾallam lazzān alwatīr* It is very difficult to learn to drive a truck.
___ *yaḷḷa* (*dugō*) *xaram min albēt* It is very difficult to come out of the house.

yam when (conj.)

yamkun ~ *y/mumkin* maybe, perhaps

yan sibbāṭ because

yān nās persons of well-to-do families

yāni šinu What do you mean?

(*y*)*ā̕ntā̕* until, when (conj.)

yaqīn, -a, -īn, -āt certain, sure

yaqqan, biyaqqin make sure or certain, prove

yárda yard (measure)

yarsanda police

yarwa Maiduguri (city in N.E. Nigeria)

yātu, yāti, -um, -in who?; who(ever) (rel.)
___ *kulla* anyone at all, whoever, everyone
___ *kulla biharrim gabīla* Everyone respects each other.

yáwwā̕ ~ *yawwā* fine, OK, great, wonderful [response to 'Welcome!']

ye self [intensifier – follows independent pronouns]
humma ___ they themselves

yibis, bēbas (be[come]) dry

yō fine, O.K., great, wonderful [response to 'Welcome!']
___ *zēn* Very well!/Yes, indeed!

yōm, (pls.) (*t*)*īyām* ~ (*ay*)*yōmāt* day
___ *alwalūda* birthday
___ *alxitāma* Day of judgment
___ *wāhid gāʾid wahada* One day he was sitting alone.
___ *-āt tinēn mā fi* He has been absent two days.

yoruba (no pl.) duck

yukūn It will be possible.

y/mumkin ~ *yamkun* maybe, perhaps

Z

zāb, buzūb move along

zabzab, bizabzib frighten, threaten, bully

zabzāb, -a, -īn, -āt threatening

zād provisions for a journey
____, *bizīd* add, increase (intr.), improve

zaffar, bizaffir be putrid

zāfir, -e, -īn, -āt putrid

zaga, bizgi irrigate, (give) water
____, *buzgu* make s.o. drink

zagal, bi/uzugul throw

zagalōna red-light district

zagga, buzugg shoot

zaggal, bizaggil throw

zaɣraṭ, bizaɣraṭ shout out of joy (usually women)

zāhir, -e, -īn, -āt obvious

zaʾaf kind of grass for making mats

zaʾʾal, bizaʾʾil make s.o. angry

zakāt alms

zāki, -ye, -yīn, -yāt honest, truthful

zakumān, -a, -īn, -āt having a cold

zālim, -e, (pl.) *zulām* cheater

zālum, -e, -īn, -āt cruel, oppressive, unjust, tyrannical (person), tyrant

z/ḍam, (pl.) *z/ḍunūb* responsibility, sin

zām, buzūm boast

zamān time; once upon a time, long ago, a long time ago; used to (v.)
____ *ana bākul* I used to eat.

zamba fraud

zamilá ~ zamīle, (coll.) *zamil* animal, beast of burden

zandūx, (pl.) *zanādīx* box

zānib, -e, -īn, -āt criminal

zann thought
____, *buzunn* think, ponder, consider

zanna ourselves

zaqaraṭat, tizaqariṭ shout out of joy (usually women)

zār, bu/izūr visit

zarab, buzrub zarra build a wall or fence around one's farm

zarāf, (pl.) *zuruffe* giraffe

zāras Zaras (p.n.f.)

zarat, buzrat swallow

zarf (no pl.) paper (for writing a letter or Koran)

zāri (no pl.) large fish net

zāria Zaria (city in N.C. Nigeria)

zarībe, (pl.) *zarāyib* enclosure, fence, wall around a farm or village

zarmax, bizarmix stink

zarr, (pl.) *zurāʾāt* farm

zarra, bizirr catch (s.o.) red-handed (in the act of doing s.t. undesirable)

zarrāni He caught me red-handed.

zāta himself, itself (m.)

zātaha herself, itself (f.)

zātak, zātik, zākku, zākkan yourself, yourselves

zāti myself

zātihin themselves (f.)

zātuhum themselves (m.)

zāwal, bizāwil vomit

zāwar, bizāwar visit

zawwad, bizawwid provide, supply, give provisions for a journey

zawwām, -a, -īn, -āt boastful

zāyim, zāyme, -īn, -āt boastful

zayyan, bizayyin shave

zayyāni, (pl.) *zayyānīn* barber

zayyar, bizayyir invite

zēn, -e, -īn, -āt good (thing), nice, all right, pleasant, kind, polite
 ___ *zēn* very good, very well

zēnaba Zenab (p.n.f.)

zēnāy right (directional adv.)
 ___, *-e, -īn, -āt* right-handed, right-hander

zētūn olive (tree)

zibde animal fat used for grooming purposes

zigēge (no pl.) package, parcel; gift, present

ziggāfá, (pl.) *zaggāfāt* bedroom in a village house

ziʾil, bizal become angry

ziyāda, (pl.) *-āt* increase, raise (in salary)
 ___ *yā giddām* advance, promotion

zōl, (pl.) *zīlān* male, man

zu zoo

zugg allēl midnight

zukumá cold (n.)

zulum cruelty, injustice, oppression

zur perjury

zūriye, (pl.) *zurāyāt* grandchild(ren), family